# STRANGE WORLDS

BIG PROBE

*Compiled by*

Pat Edwards & Wendy Body

Fife **Council**

✔ KU-419-981

Fife Council Education Department

King's Road Primary School

King's Crescent, Rosyth KY11 2RS

## Acknowledgements

We are grateful to the following for permission to reproduce copyright material: Allen & Unwin Australia Pty Ltd for an extract from *Shields of Trell* by Jenny Summerville; Andre Deutsch Ltd for the poem 'Here is the News' from *Wouldn't You Like To Know* by Michael Rosen; Oxford University Press, New Zealand, and the author's agent for an extract from *The Halfmen of O* by Maurice Gee (pub Oxford University Press and Puffin Books); Penguin Books Ltd for the story 'Flying Saucers Have Landed' from *Plays for Laughs* by Johnny Ball (Puffin Books, 1983), copyright © Johnny Ball 1983; Random House, Inc for an extract from *Star Wars: Return of the Jedi: The Storybook Based On The Movie* by Joan D Vinge. Copyright © 1983 by Lucasfilm Ltd (LFL); the author's agents for the story 'The Collecting Team' from *Alien Worlds* by Robert Silverberg © Agberg Ltd; the author, C S Youd for an extract from his book *The Lotus Caves* by John Christopher.

We have been unable to trace the copyright holder of the poem 'Space Travellers' from *Junior Poetry Workshop* by James Nimmo (pub Thomas Nelson Australia) and would appreciate any information that would enable us to do so.

We are grateful to the following for permission to reproduce photographs: Copyright by Universal Pictures, a Division of Universal City Studios, Inc. Courtesy of MCA Publishing Rights, a Division of MCA Inc., page 33 *above* (photo National Film Archive); Henson Associates Inc., 1982, page 24 (photo Ronald Grant Archive); Lucasfilm Ltd, pages 25, 31, (photos National Film Archive), 30 (photo Eva Sereny), 36, 37, 39, 41; NASA (Washington), pages 79, 82/83, 84, 85, 86, 87; Neilson-Hordell Ltd, page 29; © 1933 RKO Radio Pictures, Inc. Ren. 1960 RKO Radio Pictures, a division of RKO General, Inc., page 33 *below* (photo National Film Archive). Cover: Still from the film *Dark Crystal*, Henson Associates Inc., 1982 (photo Ronald Grant Archive).

Illustrators, other than those acknowledged with each story, include Oxford Illustrators pp.4-5; Bettina Guthridge pp.20-3; Paul Collicutt pp.24-33; John Fairbridge pp.34-5; Peter Schmidli pp.76-7; Azoo pp.88-9; Rebecca Pannell p.110; Kathy Baxendale pp.111-12.

# Contents

# SPACE TRAVELLERS' GUIDE TO THE SOLAR SYSTEM

Mercury

Venus

Earth

Mars

Jupiter

Saturn

This drawing shows the sizes of the planets in comparison with one another

Jupiter

Mercury

Venus

Earth

Mars

4

| Distances from the sun | |
| --- | --- |
| Mercury | 58 million km |
| Venus | 108 million km |
| Earth | 149 million km |
| Mars | 228 million km |
| Jupiter | 778 million km |
| Saturn | 1427 million km |
| Uranus | 2870 million km |
| Neptune | 4497 million km |
| Pluto | 5900 million km |

There are nine planets which travel around the sun. Mercury is nearest to the sun and Pluto is the farthest.

Uranus

Neptune

Pluto

Saturn

Uranus

Neptune

Pluto

# THE STRANGE WORLD OF
# ODO CLING

*Susan Ferris has been suddenly and mysteriously transported from her father's quiet farm in New Zealand to a strange and hideous land where everything is grey. Sky, hills, trees are all the colour of tin. The huge sun is black and, worst of all, she too has been turned grey — her hair and her hands; even her nails shine like chips of polished stone.*

*Before she can work out what has happened, Susan is captured by Odo Cling and his Deathguards. He is a sinister figure dressed all in leather and black iron. He is grey too, like her; except his eyes. They are red and cruel. He seems to know her. In particular, he seems to know about those strange marks on her wrist, marks which she had never understood.*

*Susan had stumbled out of a dark slimy tunnel into this strange world. But how did it happen? And how did her father's farm disappear? And where is Nick, her cousin? What's happened to him? She was with him moments ago — where is he now?*

**S**usan threw a last desperate look behind her, then was pushed roughly along by the guard at her back. She stepped down to the track and went zig-zagging through shale and stunted trees. The black sun was low in the sky. Far below, a river wound towards the fringe of a forest. She guessed Odo Cling was heading for some camp down there and hoped to reach it before night fell.

When the path levelled out she threw a glance behind her but the tunnel was hidden by the brow of the hill. The file of guards coming down made a black zed on the slope. They were, she thought, like a band of Inquisition monks going to watch someone burned at the stake. She trotted desperately after Odo Cling. He was the worst of them, but at least he had said he meant to keep her unharmed for the time being. They crossed a narrow plateau and before

starting down the slope beyond it she turned and saw the tunnel in view again. It had shrunk to an insignificant mark on the face of the cliff. She wondered how she would ever find it again if she escaped. Then she almost gave a cry. Something moved up there. It fluttered like a bird in the tunnel mouth. She could not see, she could not quite make out . . . Then the guard behind gave a hiss and sent her reeling with a thrust of his palm. They went in file down a new slope, and the tunnel was lost. She knew she would not see it again. But something had moved. She did not even know if it was human. As they went down the shaly slopes, across the plateaux, through a landscape without variation or colour, she clung to that movement as her only hope.

They walked for an hour or more. She saw she had been wrong about reaching a camp. The black sun slid down into the haze beyond the forest and still they seemed no closer to the river than when they had started. Blackness began to grow like a fog in the air. They came down a steep hill, turning among thorny trees, and at the bottom Odo Cling held up his hand.

"Here."

It was no camp, simply a place to stop. Coarse grass grew among the stones. Odo Cling sat down. He pointed. A guard forced Susan down.

"Give her water."

She was feeling dizzy and breathless and wanted time to recover, but someone thrust the neck of a flask in her mouth and she drank lukewarm water tasting of mothballs. Odo Cling was eating from a jar brought by one of his men.

"Feed her."

"No," Susan said, "I'm not hungry."

"You will eat. We have five days to march. I do not want you dying."

A hand thrust something grey at her mouth. "No." She twisted her head away. At once another guard sprang forward. He seized her jaw, forced her mouth open. The first man pushed something slimy inside. Then her mouth was forced shut. Fingers clamped her nose. She had to swallow. It felt horrible — slimy, thick, cold — but the worst part was that it had no taste. It was like swallowing pieces of greasy plastic. They fed her half a dozen, then Odo Cling said, "Enough."

She gasped and gagged for a while but the food stayed down.

"**N**ow you will sleep."

"I want to wash," she managed to say.

"Tomorrow. When we reach the river." He signed to one of his men, who took a blanket out of his pack and spread it on the ground.

"Lie on it," Cling said.

Susan obeyed. The man folded the blanket over her. She shivered. The spiky grass and stones hurt her sides.

"I can't sleep with my hands tied."

"Do you think we mean to let you escape Mixie?"

"It hurts."

"Quiet. Another word and I will have you whipped."

All around the men of the Deathguard were arranging themselves for sleep. They curled up like cats in their black robes. Two men walked silently round the rim of the camp. Two more stood at her head and feet. A night black as coal came down. Later there was a faint lightening as a moon rose behind shifting clouds. She glimpsed it from time to time and it was coloured like pewter and had markings her moon did not have. She slept a little, and woke whimpering. A guard hissed at her. Suddenly Odo Cling's face was bending over her. "I told you to sleep."

"I can't. I'm cold. I'm aching all over."

Cling made an angry sound. He fumbled at his neck. All the guards kept a little bag of something there, and sniffed at it from time to time. Cling, too, had a bag. She had seen him put it to his nose several times on the walk down from the tunnel. Now he thrust it at her face.

"No. No."

"Sniff. Then you will sleep."

"No."

He seized her hair. She cried out with pain. But the hard little bag came down under her nose and over her mouth and a carbide reek filled her and she felt herself hurled into sleep as though by a great blow on her head. For the rest of the night she dreamed hideous dreams that had no shape, that were all twisting and whirling and falling into black pits with no bottom. When she woke in the morning her face was salty with tears. She knew she could not go through another five days of this.

They fed her again and then Odo Cling had her hands untied and let her wash at a small spring in the side of the hill. Guards stood at her back with knives drawn. When they came to tie her again she said, "Please, tie my hands in front. I won't try to escape."

"No."

"I'll walk faster."

Odo Cling thought. "No tricks, Mixie." He signalled the guards. "Tie them in front." They bound her tight, eyeing the mark on her wrist. Cling seemed in a good mood. "Here." He walked to the edge of the slope and looked out over the falling land. A guard brought Susan to his side. "See," Cling pointed, "tonight we will reach the forest. Then three days to Sheercliff. Then down out of this stinking air into the glory of Darkland. There you will meet Otis Claw." He grinned. "I do not know what he plans for you Mixie, but I shall be there to enjoy it all."

Susan shivered. She tried to concentrate on the view in front. Although much of it was still in shadow, things stood out with a clarity they had lacked the night before. The forest was tar-black. It ran on and on like a huge rumpled blanket on the land. The river curved into it and vanished. She could not see the place Cling had called Sheercliff, but guessed it would be a drop in the land. The forest stopped over there and gave way to a grey murkiness, like an oily pond, spreading out on the horizon. Sunlight gleamed on it. She guessed it was a kind of smog. Underneath lay the place Odo Cling called Darkland. What was that? And who was Otis Claw? She shivered again and looked behind her. The guards were drawn up in a file, ready to move out. Beyond them the land climbed into the sky. Huge grey hills filled the horizon. Here and there the peaks of mountains rose. A dark glow showed where the sun would rise over them. The mountains ran north-east, so Darkland and Sheercliff were off to the west.

She turned to Odo Cling. "I don't know where I am or why I'm here."

"You don't need to know."

"I've got a right. You've taken me away from home."

"There is no home. And Mixies have no rights. Halfmen rule O. That is enough."

"I don't know any O. I don't belong here. I'm from Earth."

Odo Cling sneered. "Look at your wrist. You belong."

"What is it? This mark?"

"The less you know the less dangerous you are. Enough talk. March. We have a long way to go."

They started off again. Susan was third in line, behind Cling and one of the guards. She walked more easily with her hands tied in front. She began to wonder if she could dart off to one side and escape among the boulders beside the track. But the guard behind was never more than a step away. He hissed each time she turned to look at him. By midday she was exhausted. They stopped to eat and she sprawled on the ground. When a guard brought her a jar of the grey meat she ate it almost hungrily. She knew she must keep her strength up.

In the early afternoon the track was easier. It ran over a plain where the only obstacle was an occasional outcrop of rock. Susan kept up easily. She began to feel strong and made up her mind that next time she saw a chance she would try to get away. Then, if she could find a sharp stone and cut the rope round her wrists, she should have a good chance of finding her way back to the tunnel — and maybe whatever it was she had seen moving around up there would help her find her way back through the spinning dream to her own world.

They came to the edge of the plain. A long slope fell away to the river and forest. It was broken country, full of ravines and gorges and clumps of trees, and boulders sharp as knives that pointed every way. She felt elated. Surely her chance would come in there. They started down. The path dropped sharply, curving round boulders and cutting across cliff-faces. They went by tumbling streams and waterfalls. Then Susan thought she saw a perfect place. On the left the ground sloped down from the path, then dropped out of sight into a black ravine; but on the right a cleft showed in the cliff. It was full of trees and boulders, closely packed, just right for someone her size to scramble through. If she could get in there she would leave these men in their flapping robes far behind. She grinned with determination.

Odo Cling passed the cleft without a glance. The guard went past. Then Susan came to it. There was a tree bending low to the path and as she came level she took two quick steps, jumped on the trunk, ran along it like a path, and began to haul herself over the boulders. As soon as she was clear of them she would be in the cleft, and climbing, and none of the guards would get near her. There was a slapping of feet on stone, a scrambling sound of hands, a clink of knives. She heard Odo Cling screeching commands. And it was then that she saw she had misjudged. The final boulder was too steep for her. She felt for hand-holds desperately, but the surface was smooth. She looked about for ways to go. There was no time. The first guard had her. She spun around, saw his eyes burning, smelt his carbide breath, and saw his knife. She gave a scream. But he did not mean to kill her, only to hold her. His free hand came down on her wrist. He was too eager. He had forgotten. He grasped her by the wrist that had the mark.

At once a flat explosion rattled the air. Susan felt nothing. But the guard gave a shriek as the force in her picked him up and hurled him end over end like a stick, down from the boulders, over the track, on to the sloping ground. He came down like a huge black legless bird, tumbled helplessly in a spray of shingle, and vanished with a shriek into the ravine. A cry came floating up. Then there was nothing.

Susan turned again and tried to run. But in her pause a guard had scrambled up another way and stood above her. Two others came sliding along the rocks. Before she had taken half a dozen steps knives were pricking at her breast and throat. She stopped and stayed absolutely still. She saw their red eyes bulging. These men were aching to kill her.

Odo Cling stood on the path. "Tie her. Hands behind." And when that was done, "Bring her." They tumbled her down from the boulders. She fell on her knees at Odo Cling's feet.

"So Mixie, you have killed one of my men. I shall make you suffer."

"I didn't mean to kill him."

"I should throw you down to join him. I should throw you to the jackals."

"I don't care what you do."

"You will care." He flicked his whip at her cheek. She felt it burn like fire. He laughed. "That is just a taste. And now we will see how you like travelling in a throttle." He jerked with the whip and a guard brought a leather collar from his pack. It had ropes running through it. He placed it over Susan's head and pulled it tight on her throat. A guard in front took one rope and a guard

behind the other. "On your feet, Mixie. Any tricks and either one of them can throttle you."

So they walked through the afternoon. They went through gorges, down the sides of cliffs on paths that would have troubled a goat, tracked across shingle slides, walked on slimy stone beside black streams, and all the time Susan felt that wicked collar pressing on her windpipe. She took care with every step. One slip and the guards would choke her.

The sun was going down when they reached the river. They crossed by a ford and made camp on the edge of the forest. The trees were close-packed and the dark in there was more intense than any Susan had ever seen. She wondered if tomorrow they would travel in the forest. But she had no strength left to be frightened. She drank when a flask was thrust into her mouth and ate more lumps of slimy meat. Then she lay down and tried to sleep. She knew better than to ask Odo Cling to have her hands untied or have the collar taken from her neck. The guards at her head and feet had the ropes tied round their waists. Every time she swallowed she felt the leather pressing on her throat. She tried not to move, tried to breathe softly. Whatever happened, she did not want Odo Cling pressing his horrible sniffing-bag under her nose.

She managed to doze for a while, and woke when the guards were changing. She lay still as everything settled down. Now and then distant animal cries came from the forest. Once a bird like a morepork sounded close. Tears ran down her face. She would never hear real moreporks again, or see fantails, or see her mother and father, or her dopey cousin, Nicholas Quinn. She tried to wipe her face on her blanket. The guard at her head gave his rope a jerk. Then he leaned down and loosened the collar so she could breathe. After a while she dozed again.

She woke with the moon on her face. Grey light filled the campsite. Boulders gleamed in the grass and the trunks of the trees in the forest stood out like an army of soldiers. Something had woken her. Cautiously she turned her head and looked about. The men wrapped in their robes slept without moving. Odo Cling lay only an arm's length away. His breath sang horribly in his nose. Watchmen paced by the forest and river. The guards at her head and feet stood still as stone. Everything was normal. Yet something was wrong. She felt it. Or perhaps something was right. She felt a thrill in her blood at the thought. Then the answer came — a birdcall from the forest.

"Morepork." A long pause. "Morepork." She felt herself almost choking with delight and anguish.

There was no mistake: a morepork, a bird from her world. But somehow she knew it was more than that — she knew it was a message for her alone. Someone from her world was out in the bush, making that call. Someone was coming to rescue her.

She lay still as a cat. Half an hour passed. The watchmen paced. The guards breathed and sighed, exchanged a grunt. Everything was still. Then the moon went behind a cloud. Nothing changed. Rustlings came as men turned in their sleep. The moon slid out again. And something *had* changed. She saw it at once. The watchman by the river, the watchman by the forest, were not there. And all about, motionless and low upon the grass were boulders in the shapes of crouching men. Her guards had not seen. Knowing she was roped, they stood and dozed, hands upon their waists.

Susan held her breath. She felt if she made the smallest movement Odo Cling would wake, the guards would spring into action. She kept her eyes on the boulders. None of them moved. Yet she knew they were men, and knew that they had come to rescue her. She turned her eyes to see the moon. A cloud thick as oil, heavy as an elephant, moved ponderously down on it. A minute more, then the night would turn black as soot, her rescuers would come.

Moving slow as treacle, the cloud blotted out the moon. Again a darkness heavy as wool came on Susan's eyes. She strained to hear, but the stirrings, the faint rustlings, seemed no more than normal night-time noises. When she had almost given up hope, the guard at her head gave a small grunt of surprise. Then he sighed. The man at her feet made a quick movement – she heard the oily scrape of a knife half-drawn from its scabbard – then he sighed too. Straining her ears, she heard mouse-like movements, whisperings of cloth. A voice breathed in the hair about her face, making it stir. "Be still . . . You are safe." She felt hands at her throat, loosening the collar, lifting it off.

"Thank —"

"Shsh."

A knife worked on the rope binding her wrists. In a moment she was free. She tried to sit up.

"No," the voice breathed. "Stay here. We will come."

Something crept away. Then she heard faint noises among the sleeping guards. She wondered if her rescuers were moving among them, killing them perhaps. The thought made her feel sick. But in a moment the moon rolled out from behind its cloud and she saw half a dozen small figures, no taller than children, darting among the guards, pressing something to the face of each. Something, she guessed, that knocked them out the way Odo Cling's bag had knocked her out.

She strained her eyes to see who the newcomers were. But the light was too dull. All she could see was that they wore robes of a lighter colour than the Deathguards. They moved as neatly as fish darting in a pond. In a moment their job was done. All the guards were lying stiff and helpless as bales of hay. They laughed, the first normal sound Susan had heard, and started back towards her, pushing the hoods back from their faces.

"Well, Susan Ferris, you are safe. Now we must get away from here."

She stood up. Her knees creaked. She felt like laughing. But as she tottered, one of her rescuers made a sudden dart. He gave a cry, "Look out." She saw a black movement at her side and felt an arm strong as fencing wire lock on her throat. Odo Cling's voice screeched at her ear, like a saw grating on a nail.

**B**ack! Back, you vermin of the woods." She saw the gleam of a knife, felt it pricking at the base of her throat. "Back, I say."

Her rescuers had halted. They stood in a knot, helplessly. Odo Cling laughed. "Did you think you could defeat Odo Cling, the Executive Officer? One move and the Mixie dies. I say it, Odo Cling, Doer of Deeds." He screeched again, more a scream of triumph than a laugh. "Did you think you had knocked me out with your stink-pads? I am immune. I have taken the cure. No stink-pad works against the great Odo Cling. I lay quiet till I saw my chance. And now I have her. I have the Mixie. And you will stay where you are till my men wake up. Then we will have some sport."

One of the rescuers shook his head. He seemed dazed, he seemed to have shrunk. "I'm sorry, Susan."

"How do you know my name?"

"Quiet!" Odo Cling screamed. His arm tightened round her throat. She managed to smile. She was calm, not the least bit frightened. She knew exactly what she was going to do.

"Don't take any notice of Odo Cling. He's not very clever. He's forgotten the most important thing."

"Quiet, Mixie. I shall cut your tongue out."

"This," Susan said. Almost lazily she raised her arm and laid the mark on her wrist on Odo Cling's hand. The detonation so close to her ears made her head seem to split in two. Odo Cling was torn from her so roughly that she staggered and almost fell. But she saw him go spinning high in the air, thin legs poking at angles, and saw him crash down in a tangle over the bodies of his sleeping guards. He lay still.

"That's what he forgot," Susan said. Then she sat down. She felt rather faint suddenly.

A figure came running from the forest. He wore a robe like the ones her rescuers wore. But his hood was back, she saw his face. He ran through the Deathguards and jumped over Odo Cling. Susan stood up. She took a step towards him. He grabbed her in his arms and hugged her until she could hardly breathe.

"Susan. You're all right. Thank God."

She started to cry. It was good just to be able to cry. She let her tears run on to his shoulder. "Nick. Oh, Nick. Where on earth did you come from?"

*Text by Maurice Gee*
*Illustrated by Gaston Vanzet*

# Conversation with a Confused ALIEN

| | |
|---|---|
| **Alien** | From . . . spaceship . . . your planet . . . mostly blue. Why? |
| *Earthling* | Ah, that's easy my alien friend. My planet is blue because three-quarters of it is covered by water. |
| | |
| **Alien** | Is water . . . on . . . surface only? |
| *Earthling* | My planet has two kinds of water. What you see is mostly saltwater. There is freshwater too, in rivers and lakes and underground. Earth is like a giant sponge. |
| | |
| **Alien** | How long . . . water . . . been there? |
| *Earthling* | Billions of years! In fact, water began collecting in the basins of the Earth's crust while my planet was forming. |
| | |
| **Alien** | Have you . . . same amount . . . water . . . on planet Earth today, as . . . millions . . . years ago? |
| *Earthling* | I think so, but it's being used more by people and we are running out of water in some parts of the world. We have to be careful about saving it. |

I'm a UMO!

what's that?

An unidentified marine object.

**Water, water, everywhere.**

| | |
|---|---|
| **Alien** | Could same water . . . you drink now . . . have been drunk . . . by dinosaur . . . 150 million years ago? |
| *Earthling* | A good thought my friend! And yes, it could be! Water is recycled over and over again thanks to Mother Nature. It evaporates from the oceans and the land, forms clouds and comes down again as rain or snow. It may run into the rivers or soak deep down underground and stay there for thousands of years, but it will sooner or later be recycled again. That's called the *hydrologic cycle*. |
| **Alien** | Water . . . very exciting! For what do you use it? |
| *Earthling* | Well, all living things on our planet need water to survive. We use it in our homes. We wash in it, cook with it, drink it, hose the garden with it, swim in it . . . |
| **Alien** | You dirty it! Do you have problems? |
| *Earthling* | Unfortunately we do. A lot of people don't seem to care. They seem to think water will last forever. Even in our homes we pour cooking oil down our sinks. |

21

| | |
|---|---|
| **Alien** | Is that . . . only way you . . . damage water? |
| *Earthling* | I'm afraid the answer is 'no'. Poisonous wastes from many different industries can leak into our water supplies. Once water is poisoned, it's almost impossible to purify it again. |
| **Alien** | Has no . . . Earthling . . . corrected it? |
| *Earthling* | Yes. Many factories use water to make their products and some of these factories clean up their dirty water so they can use it again. And now our councils and governments have laws making it an offence to pollute our water, though it's a bit hard to police. |
| **Alien** | How much water . . . Earthlings drink? |
| *Earthling* | In my life, I will drink enough water to fill over 300 bathtubs! |
| **Alien** | Amazing! How much water is . . . salty? How much is fresh? |
| *Earthling* | Most is saltwater. For every bathtub of saltwater, there is only about 2 litres of liquid freshwater. |
| **Alien** | You should save . . . freshwater? |
| *Earthling* | Yes! And we're also trying to increase the quantity. Scientists are experimenting with ways to turn seawater into freshwater. |

**Alien**    Do Earthlings . . . ever fight . . . for water?

**Earthling**    Yes, throughout history people have fought wars over water rights and civilisations have flourished in areas which have fresh water. If you felt like being nasty to someone, you could always pour poison down their wells . . .

**Alien**    Ugh! Where else is . . . water?

**Earthling**    A lot of our food is made up of water. An egg is 74% water, a piece of steak is 73% water, watermelon is 92% water and even my body is 65% water!

**Alien**    Do Earthlings . . . use more water than . . . long ago?

**Earthling**    Yes, definitely! Because of the way we live one person can easily flush 100 litres of water down a toilet everyday, use another 100 litres to water the garden and much more to fill the swimming pool, and 100 litres or so to wash ourselves and our clothes . . .

**Alien**    Stop! Stop! What are you doing to your planet? Next it will shrink . . . or sink!

**Earthling**    Um . . . well . . . you see Alien . . . um . . . it has sunk in places. In central California, so much water has been taken out of the ground it has sunk 3 metres!

**Alien**    That is it! I leave! Bye Earthling!

*Margarette Thomas-Cochran*

Which brings us to the watertight conclusion . . . without water we'd be SUNK!

23

# SPECIAL EFFECTS

Very few films, for
cinema or television, are made
today without the assistance of a
special effects team, who use their skill to
trick the audience into believing that they are seeing
something which really they aren't.

**MODELS**

Monsters in films are often 'played' by models which have been built
carefully in the film studio. They are often very big. In the film *Dark
Crystal* all the characters were played by puppets.

The director, Steven Spielberg, looking at a model set for *Raiders of the Lost Ark*

© Henson Associates, Inc., 1982

It is often too expensive to create a full sized set, so models are made. Model sets need to be constructed carefully and in great detail in order to look realistic.

Models are often used when crashes or explosions are needed, for example plane crashes in war films. A model plane is made of light balsa wood which breaks up on impact. It can contain safe explosives which go off to make the crash look realistic.

25

# CAMERA SPECIAL EFFECTS

If you want to add extra detail to a room or a view, you can do this by placing a sheet of glass in front of the camera, and painting the extra details onto the glass. The camera has to be lined up very carefully to make sure that everything matches.

Occasionally a matte shot is used as a way of getting more details into one picture. A sheet of black card is put in front of the camera so that only part of the picture is recorded. The film is then rewound and the black card moved to block the part of the film that has already been used. This method can be used, for example, if an actor needs to appear twice in the same frame of film, (perhaps playing identical twins).

26

## SCENIC PROJECTION

Outdoor scenes can be filmed cheaply in the studio by projecting a photograph of the background onto a screen, and filming the actors as they perform in front of this screen. The photograph can be projected from in front of the screen or from behind: it depends on the kind of screen used.

## BACK PROJECTION

large mirror (this helps cut down the distance needed from the projector to the screen)

projector

stage

camera

## FRONT PROJECTION

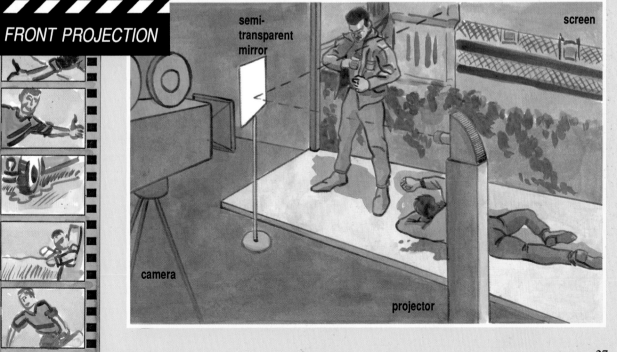

semi-transparent mirror

screen

camera

projector

You need to show two people on a magic carpet flying over the rooftops at night. One way of doing this is to combine two images electronically using the 'chromakey' technique. One camera takes two people sitting on a carpet. The carpet can be on a blue support against a completely blue background or on a blue floor. The other camera takes the rooftops at night. The electronics in the vision mixer are programmed to 'switch' when the colour blue is seen. Wherever there is blue on the first picture, the machine will substitute the second picture. So the blue background will be replaced with the rooftops at night. If you have someone dressed totally in blue, then they can move things but be invisible on the end result!

Chromakey is often used for news broadcasts where the reader is seen in front of a map or diagram.

28

# LABORATORY SPECIAL EFFECTS

Special effects can be created in the laboratory during printing, using an optical printing machine. This machine has a projector and a camera facing each other, so that while the developed film is being fed through the projector and rephotographed by the camera, many sorts of change can be made to the pictures. The pictures can be enlarged or reduced by moving the camera nearer to or further away from the projector. By missing out some of the film frames during printing, the action can be speeded up, to make it look more exciting or funny. It can be slowed down by printing some frames more than once. Comic shots of action in reverse can be made by running the projector backwards so that the pictures are printed in reverse order.

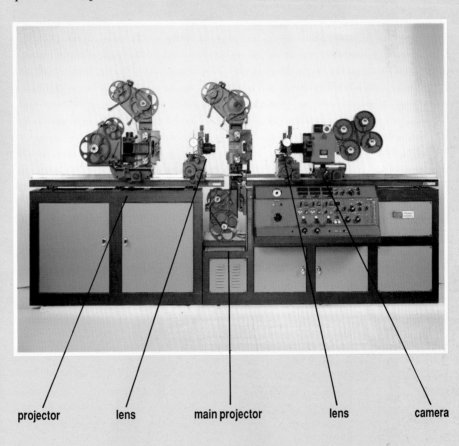

projector    lens    main projector    lens    camera

# STUNTS

Stunts are special effects achieved in a variety of ways to convince the watching audience that dangerous actions are taking place. Film actors and actresses nowadays do more of their stunts themselves, but for sequences that they do not feel confident to do, stunt men and women, who have completed a very tough training, are employed. For the final scene in a chase, if there is a crash or an explosion, shots can be taken using dummies. The car is operated by remote control and is often fitted with explosives to give a spectacular effect on crashing.

Stunt from *Indiana Jones and the Temple of Doom*

Most guns used in filming are 'dummies'. Real weapons are only seen in 'still' close ups. For fight scenes a gun which fires blanks is used.

Knives used in fights can be made from foam plastic or rubber. Daggers with blades that can be pulled back into the handle are also used. As the blade is pulled into the handle, imitation blood contained in the handle flows down a tube in the centre of the blade.

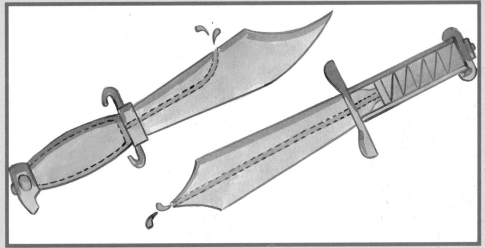

Sword fight from *Indiana Jones and the Temple of Doom*

Fire scenes are best filmed out in the open. But if they have to be done in the studio, there are several ways of creating the impression of a big fire without being too dangerous! Smoke lit with bright lights at floor level, can make it look as if the fire is much bigger than it actually is. A flame drum — a transparent plastic drum with strips painted black and lit from the inside — gives the flickering effect to the fire. Flame forks — metal tubes attached via a hose to a bottled gas supply — are used to provide controllable flame. If they are carefully positioned, it can look as if furniture is on fire when in fact it isn't.

# FAMOUS FILMS

Here are some scenes from famous films well known for their special effects. Can you work out how the effects were done?

A scene from *ET* (1982)

A scene from *King Kong* (1933)

# Human Rights Day

**When is it?**     10th December

**What is it?**

Human Rights Day grew out of a declaration produced by the United Nations on
10 December 1948. It was felt that an international definition of the rights of men
and women was needed so that countries everywhere would have goals for their
governments to work towards. Many new countries have used the Declaration as
a guide when shaping their constitutions and it has influenced many other nations,
helping to stamp out slavery and forced labour and making everyone more aware
of the rights of women and children in particular.

**What does the Declaration say?**

*Governments must protect*:

- the right of individuals to life, liberty and security
- the right of everyone to an education and to equality before the law
- the right of each person to move about freely, to worship as he or she pleases, to associate freely with other people, and to have access to information in a search for understanding
- the right of everyone to be a citizen of a country and to work under favourable conditions with equal pay for equal work
- the right to marry and raise a family

**Why should we observe it?**

So much of the world's history revolves around the concept of the freedom of the individual to choose how she or he wants to live. The Declaration is considered one of the finest accomplishments of the United Nations. It set a goal for everyone to work for, for many believe there will be no peace on earth until every individual has these basic rights.

*"If men and women are in chains anywhere in the world, then freedom is endangered everywhere."*

John F Kennedy

# THE DARK SIDE OF THE FORCE

LONG AGO, in a galaxy far away, the leaders of the Rebellion are fighting against the Emperor who is ruler of the evil Galactic Empire.

The Rebellion is led by a young pilot named Luke Skywalker and his friends. Luke is also a Jedi which means he has mysterious powers which come from the Force.

Darth Vader is on the side of the Emperor. He controls the Emperor's Imperial soldiers. He too has mysterious powers that come from the Force, but he uses them for evil. He can use the dark side of the Force better than anyone ex-cept for the Emperor. He can kill a man just by looking at him. He can make his subjects do whatever he wishes. No one can resist him. And he is also Luke Sky-walker's father!

Luke has just been told the awful truth, how his father was lured to the dark side of the Force by the Emperor and the good man that he used to be was lost forever. So now Luke knows that he and his father are enemies and most likely they will have to fight each other, to death!

It wasn't long before Luke ran into a squad of Imperial soldiers. He surren-

dered to them without a fight, knowing they would take him to Darth Vader.

Darth Vader stood waiting on the deck of the Imperial landing platform. His troops brought Luke to him and then left them alone together.

"The Emperor is expecting you," the Dark Lord said. "He believes you will turn to the dark side."

"I know . . . Father." Luke searched for some glimpse of a face behind Vader's mask. His heart was beating very fast.

"So you have finally accepted the truth."

Luke nodded. "I have accepted the truth that you were once Anakin Sky-walker, my father."

"That name no longer has any meaning for me," Vader said.

"It is the name of your true self!" Luke insisted. "You have only forgotten. I know there is good in you. That is why you won't kill me. That is why you won't take me to the Emperor now. Come away with me, Father." He moved closer to Vader. *You must have good in you*, he thought, *or how can I?*

Vader ignited Luke's lightsabre and held it between them. He shook his head. His breath hissed loudly in the silence. At last he said, "You do not know the power of the dark side. I must obey my master." Vader knew that if it was necess-ary, the Emperor would sacrifice him without pity to turn his son to the dark side. But his life, his very soul, were no longer his own.

"I will not join you," Luke said. "You will have to kill me."

"If that is your destiny," Vader answered tonelessly.

"Search your feelings, Father!" Luke cried. "I feel the conflict within you. Let go of your hate."

Vader extinguished the lightsabre and signalled for the guards. "It is too late for me, my son."

Luke bowed his head. He wondered whether the conflict he had felt was only within his own heart. "Then my father is truly dead."

Darth Vader took him away to meet the Emperor.

On the *Death Star*, Luke and Darth Vader entered the Emperor's throne room.

"Welcome, young Skywalker," the Emperor said. "I've been expecting you. Soon you will call *me* Master, as your father does."

Luke stared defiantly at the shrunken, grotesque being who had corrupted his father. "You won't make me join the dark side. Soon I will die, and so will you."

The Emperor laughed. "Do you mean because the Rebel fleet will attack us? We are quite safe from them here."

Luke was stunned. How did the Emperor know about the attack? But he only said, "You are too confident. That makes you weak."

"Your faith in your friends is *your* weakness," the Emperor said. "They are walking into a trap. And so is the Rebel fleet. Your friends will never destroy the shield generator. An entire legion of my troops is waiting for them." He pointed out the wide window at the moon.

Luke couldn't hide his fear this time as he thought of his friends. He looked at his lightsabre, which Darth Vader had given to the Emperor.

"Everything is happening just as I planned." The Emperor smiled. "The deflector shield will still be operating when the Rebel fleet arrives. And that is only the beginning of my surprise . . .

From here you will watch the final destruction and the end of your pitiful Rebellion."

He held the laser sword out to Luke. "You want this, don't you? Go ahead — take your Jedi weapon and kill me. Give in to your anger. The more hatred you feel, the closer you come to joining the dark side."

Luke's hands opened and closed helplessly as he tried to decide what to do. He must kill the Emperor, or his friends and the Rebellion would be lost. But if striking the Emperor down meant turning to the dark side .... "No, never," he said. He would not surrender like his father had — he would not!

"You must. It is your destiny." The Emperor held out the lightsabre. "You, like your father, are now ... mine."

The Emperor, Darth Vader, and Luke watched the battle rage out in space.

"As you can see, my young apprentice," the Emperor said, "your friends have failed. Now watch the fire power of this fully armed battle station." He put Luke's lightsabre nearby, where Luke could reach it easily.

Luke turned, numb with horror. The *Death Star's* weapons were fully operational. And now the Emperor was about to use its terrible power against the helpless Rebel fleet! Luke looked back out the window just in time to see a deadly beam of energy shoot out from the *Death Star*. The beam destroyed a Rebel Star Cruiser as if it were a mere fly.

The Emperor's high, piercing laughter was the only sound in the *Death Star's* throne room. "Your fleet is lost," he said to Luke, "and your friends will all die."

Luke's eyes were full of rage. His lightsabre began to shake where it lay as he fought his own battle with the dark side of himself.

The Emperor smiled. "Good," he whispered. "Strike me down with your hatred, and join the dark side."

Luke could stop himself no longer. The lightsabre flew into his hand. But as he struck at the Emperor, Darth Vader's laser sword blocked his blow. Luke turned to fight his father at last.

In the throne room Luke and his father fought their own desperate battle as the Emperor watched. Luke's powers were as strong as his father's now, and just as deadly. At last Luke's father stumbled and dropped his lightsabre. Luke stood above him, ready to attack.

"Go on!" the Emperor hissed. "Let the hate flow through you."

Luke looked up at the Emperor, suddenly realising that he was doing just what the evil ruler wanted him to do. The Emperor wanted him to kill his own father. That was the unforgivable act that would make him belong to the dark side forever. Luke lowered his sword.

Vader attacked Luke again, forcing Luke to defend himself. Luke took cover behind the Emperor's throne. "I will not fight you, Father. Take my weapon." He threw his lightsabre onto the floor. "I do not believe you will destroy me."

Vader picked up the weapon. "Give yourself to the dark side, Luke," he said. "It is the only way you can save your friends. I know your thoughts. Your feelings for them are strong."

He knew his son's emotions. He knew exactly how to stir Luke's anger and fear.

"Never!" Luke cried. His lightsabre flew back to him, and he attacked his father harder than before. Sparks flew and the air crackled with energy. He struck the lightsabre from Vader's grasp

and it flew into the deep shaft at the center of the room. Luke saw his father's useless, broken mechanical hand.

He looked down at his own artificial hand. *I'm becoming just like him*, he thought. He held his lightsabre at his father's throat.

"Kill him!" cried the Emperor. "Take your father's place at my side."

Luke looked at the Emperor and back at his father. Then he made the choice that he had been preparing for. He hurled his sabre away. "No," he said. "I will never turn to the dark side. You have failed, Your Highness. I am a Jedi, as my father was before me."

The Emperor's face twisted with hate. "Then if you will not be turned," he said, "you will be destroyed!" Blinding bolts of energy shot from his hands and struck Luke down.

Darth Vader crawled, like a wounded animal, to the Emperor's side.

Luke lay still under the Emperor's blinding energy bolts. The ruler of the dark side smiled in triumph. He was sure that the young Jedi was dead at last. "Young fool!" he hissed. "You were no match for the power of the dark side. You have paid the price for failing to see that." He moved to stand over Luke's body.

But suddenly Vader leaped to his feet and grabbed the Emperor from behind. The Emperor struck out at him wildly. Energy bolts shot from his hands, but they went out of control. The white lightning struck Darth Vader, flowing down over his black cape like rain.

Calling up all of his strength, Vader carried the Emperor to the pit at the centre of the room and threw him into it. Far down in the pit the Emperor's body exploded.

Wounded by the terrible blasts of energy, Darth Vader swayed in the rush of wind at the edge of the pit. Luke pulled his father away to safety. Then father and son lay side by side, too weak to move.

"Go on, my son," his father whispered. "Leave me."

"No," Luke said. "I've got to save you!"

"You already have, Luke."

Luke shook his head. "Father, I won't leave you." His voice trembled. The sound of explosions was getting nearer.

Darth Vader pulled him close. "Luke, help me take this mask off."

"You'll die," Luke protested.

"Nothing can stop that now. Just once, let me face you without it. Let me look on you with my own eyes."

Slowly Luke took off his father's mask. Beneath it he saw the face of a sad old man, whose eyes were full of love.

"It's too late, Luke, too late!" his father gasped. "I want to die. I could not bear to live on like this in your world. . . . Save yourself!" And Darth Vader, Anakin Skywalker . . . Luke's father, died.

Return of the Jedi *story by George Lucas, adapted by Joan D. Vinge*

# FLYING Saucers Have Landed

Cast of characters:

AGNES
BERYL        two old ladies

[AGNES and BERYL are knitting and talking.]

AGNES: Well, there I was, doing me sprouts and looking out of my kitchen window, when it just came down in the back garden.

BERYL: What? Your washing line?

AGNES: No . . . this flying saucer.

BERYL: Oh.

AGNES: Just behind my dustbin it was, and this green man gets out.

BERYL: What? Out of your dustbin?

AGNES: No. Out of the saucer.

BERYL: Oh.

AGNES: Anyway, he comes up to the back door and knocks.

BERYL: Washing powder, was it?

AGNES: What?

BERYL: Was he selling washing powder?

AGNES: No . . .

BERYL: Tide.

AGNES: What?

BERYL: I wash in Tide.

AGNES: Me too . . . It's too cold out tide. Anyway, he says, "Me . . . space . . . Take me to your leader."

BERYL: Bold.

AGNES: Well, he was . . . yes.

BERYL: No . . . I sometimes use Bold. [*She smoothes her skirt*.] I washed this in Bold.

AGNES: It's not very white.

BERYL: Started out green.

AGNES: Fancy.

BERYL: Plain green.

AGNES: He was green.

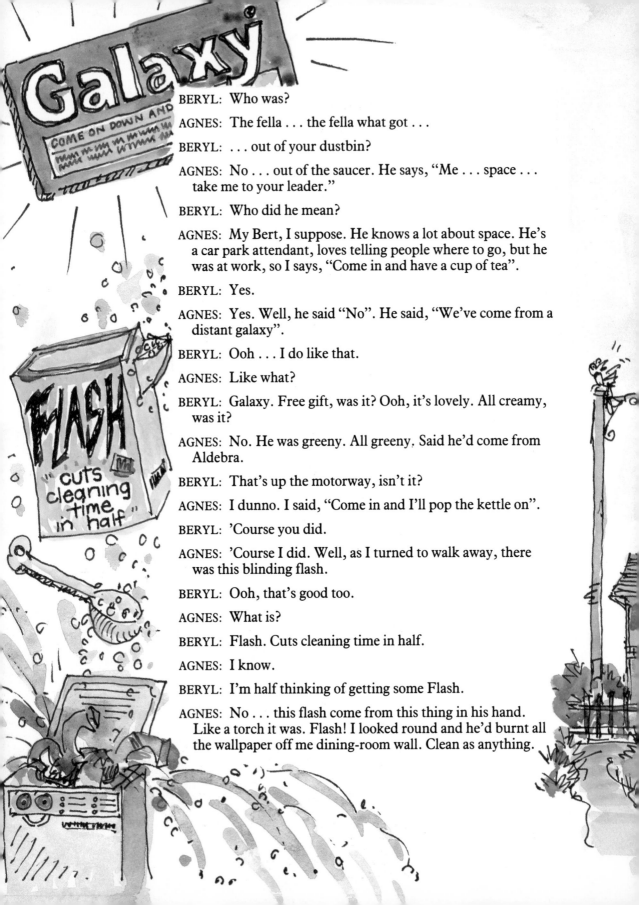

BERYL: Who was?

AGNES: The fella . . . the fella what got . . .

BERYL: . . . out of your dustbin?

AGNES: No . . . out of the saucer. He says, "Me . . . space . . . take me to your leader."

BERYL: Who did he mean?

AGNES: My Bert, I suppose. He knows a lot about space. He's a car park attendant, loves telling people where to go, but he was at work, so I says, "Come in and have a cup of tea".

BERYL: Yes.

AGNES: Yes. Well, he said "No". He said, "We've come from a distant galaxy".

BERYL: Ooh . . . I do like that.

AGNES: Like what?

BERYL: Galaxy. Free gift, was it? Ooh, it's lovely. All creamy, was it?

AGNES: No. He was greeny. All greeny. Said he'd come from Aldebra.

BERYL: That's up the motorway, isn't it?

AGNES: I dunno. I said, "Come in and I'll pop the kettle on".

BERYL: 'Course you did.

AGNES: 'Course I did. Well, as I turned to walk away, there was this blinding flash.

BERYL: Ooh, that's good too.

AGNES: What is?

BERYL: Flash. Cuts cleaning time in half.

AGNES: I know.

BERYL: I'm half thinking of getting some Flash.

AGNES: No . . . this flash come from this thing in his hand. Like a torch it was. Flash! I looked round and he'd burnt all the wallpaper off me dining-room wall. Clean as anything.

BERYL: Never did like that wallpaper.

AGNES: I know. All gone it was. Would have taken Bert a fortnight.

BERYL: I didn't know Flash was good for stripping wallpaper.

AGNES: No . . . Anyway, I turned round to say "Thank you", you know, polite like, and there he was getting back in his saucer and whoosh . . . he was gone.

BERYL: Just like that?

AGNES: Just like that. Never touched his tea.

BERYL: Funny.

AGNES: I thought that. I thought that's funny. Then I thought perhaps they was told what we was told when we were kids.

BERYL: What's that?

AGNES: You know, they always told us, "Whatever you do, never drink tea out of your saucer".

BERYL: That's right. Manners, innit?

*Written by Johnny Ball*
*Illustrated by Bettina Guthridge*

# · T H E ·
# BUBBLE

*The year is 2068. People are living on the moon, inside a huge transparent dome known as the Bubble.*

*It's a strange world of autocabins and robots instead of buses and bus drivers, stylos and plastic instead of biros and paper. But some things haven't changed . . . school for instance!*

Marty had to go all the way across the Bubble every morning, since school and his parents' apartment were both on the perimeter but almost exactly opposite. This did not present much of a problem: he only had to walk a hundred yards to pick up an autocabin. After that he punched his destination on the dial and the robots took over, swinging the cabin out on to the overhead cable and plotting the course which would take him most directly to the school depot. He had timed it once at twenty and a half minutes, and knew it would

never vary by more than seconds. It could have been a bore but he usually had enough homework held over to pass the time. The dial panel served as a desk; fairly stable except when the cabin swung out on to a new line with a jerk that sent his stylo skittering across the plastic. That sometimes meant blanking out several lines and rewriting them.

Morning was Earth-time, of course. The sun took fourteen days to arc its way across the sky above the Bubble, its glare reduced but not eliminated by the film sprayed on the inside of the huge transparent dome, and then for another fourteen days there was night, the stars and the bright globe of Earth surrounded by the deep blackness of space. That was how it was now but the long lunar night was approaching its end. Tomorrow the sun would be up.

A minute before the journey's end the dial pinged softly at him. Marty set about gathering his things. He looked out of the side and saw a boy from his class, Ben Trillici, in a cabin that was on a line converging with his towards the school run-in. There was some fun in gauging which would hit the relay first and slide through while the robot controls held the second cabin back. His was the one that made it, and he gave a thumbs-up sign and grinned. Other cabins were coming in and he checked them over to see if Paul was in one. He was not, though. Marty's guess was that he was already in school; he himself was a couple of minutes later than usual.

It was only at assembly that he realized that Paul must be away. He was surprised at that. They had visiphoned the previous evening about a problem in Maths, and he had seemed O.K. then. Moon-sickness, of course, could come on you pretty quickly. (Even after nearly fifty years of people living in the Bubble the doctors did not understand it completely: they said it was partly a disturbance of the inner ear, partly psychological.) It would have to be Moon-sickness. Owing to the barrier precautions and the isolation there were no other forms of illness. In films he had seen people on Earth suffering from things like 'flu and head colds, and wondered what it must be like to have to cough and sneeze like that.

The first class was History. They were doing the Roman Empire and Mr Milligan, the teacher, ran a reconstruct film on the screen. You saw a Roman family on the day of a Triumph, watched the yawning slaves prepare breakfast as the deep blue sky paled behind the roofs of the villa, heard the creak of ox-cart wheels in the narrow streets where the stone, through the long years, had worn into deep ruts. The family itself consisted of father and mother and five children, two boys and three girls. One of the boys was about Marty's age. He ate figs and crusty bread for breakfast, washing it down with watered wine, and was dressed in a toga which he had just become old enough to wear. Dawn had broken over the city of Rome, and the sun was a soft gleaming gold in powder blue.

Marty let his gaze stray from the scene to the windows of the class-room. Mr Milligan had not blanked them; teachers rarely did during the lunar night. They looked through the transparent wall of the Bubble to the plain and distant mountains. Nothing moved or changed there. In the brightness of Earthlight one saw the stretch of flat blackness and the far-away jagged peaks. One or two of the high points dazzled white; first signs of a very different kind of dawn.

He came back to the film. With the sound-track muted, Mr Milligan was pointing out things of which they ought to take special note: the atrium with its tinkling fountain, the triclinium with couches along three sides of the great dining-table. Then the family set out, attended by slaves, for the Senate stand from which they would watch the procession. The girls and their mother rode in litters but the Senator and his sons walked through the colourful and now crowded streets. In schools on Earth, Marty gathered, reconstruct films gave you the smell of the scene in addition to sight and sound. He had asked his father why this was not done on the Moon — was it a technical problem? Not technical, his father had said, but a matter of policy. Smell was the most powerful of all the senses, and they did not think it advisable.

English followed. They were on the late Nineteenth Century Romantic poets. Mrs Kahn read Swinburne to them:

> The full stream feeds on flower of rushes,
> Ripe grasses trammel the travelling foot,
> The faint fresh flame of the young year flushes
> From leaf to flower, and flower to fruit;
> And flower and fruit are as gold and fire,
> And the oat is heard above the lyre,
> And the hoofed heel of the satyr crushes
> The chestnut husk and the chestnut root . . .

Streams, he thought — rushes, grasses standing high by a river side and full of flowers, trees breaking into leaf in spring after a long winter. . . . He knew what they were. He had seen them on television and the cinema screen. He had even seen one fantasy film in which satyrs ran wild through a sunlit glade.

He felt a bit lost at break. Paul and he usually gossiped about TV, or continued one of their interminable games of chess, or just sat about idly and companionably. They kept more or less to themselves. Although everybody knew everybody in the Bubble, people made one or two friends and stuck to them. This morning Marty was on his own. So was Steve du Cros, but this was usual. He was an orphan, both his parents having been killed in a launch explosion when he was five or six, and a loner. He was not much liked and gave the impression of not minding that: he had a sharp tongue. The teachers were not enthusiastic about him either. He often broke rules and always gave the impression that he might be just going to.

Then, with break almost over, Marty saw Paul come in at the door. All Lunarites (the name given to those who had been born on the Moon) were taller than they would have been on Earth, but Paul was more so than most — a six-footer at fourteen. He had a thin gangling frame and a face that was ugly except when he smiled. That was his usual expression though, and he smiled now catching sight of Marty. But there was something else in his look, something odd.

Marty said: "How is it? I thought you must have the sickness."

Paul shook his head. "I'm fine."

"Then how come you missed the first two classes? Not that there was anything to miss."

"I had to see old Sherrin. Dad brought me in."

Sherrin was the Principal. Marty asked curiously:

"What about? Flunking Physics in the last exams?"

"No."

There was something which he seemed both eager and reluctant to tell. Marty said impatiently:

"Then what?"

"My folks have decided that . . . They're sending me down."

Sending down meant only one thing, one destination: the globe lighting the black sky above their heads. Marty could not believe it. He said:

"But why?"

Paul shrugged. "Some medical stuff."

"And when?"

"Next flight."

"That's . . ."

"Yes," Paul said. "Next week."

Marty thought about it in the cabin going back, about the whole business of living in the Bubble and what it meant. Those who came here did not go on home leave: the cost of transporting a human being across a quarter of a million miles, although less than it had once been, was still fantastic. You contracted, usually in your early twenties, for twenty-five years' service. At the end of that time you retired to Earth, with enough money to make your retirement years easy, even luxurious.

This meant living for a quarter of a century under the unnatural artificial conditions which the Moon enforced. As much as possible was done to make them tolerable. There was family life, for instance. Men and women were recruited in roughly equal numbers, with a preference for married couples or those engaged to be married. They could have children, though large families were discouraged. The children grew up in the Bubble never knowing anything else except at second hand on a screen. At any time after early childhood parents could, if they chose, decide to send them down — send them back to Earth. The snag was that the trip was one-way and once-only. Parents and child would not see each other again, except on the expensive inter-world visiphone link, until the end of the parents' tour of duty. For Lunarites, sending down also involved several weeks of conditioning in a special unit, with gravity slowly built up to full Earth strength and muscles trained to bear the extra weight.

Marty, like Paul, was fourteen. He had been born in the Bubble five years after his mother and father had come to the Moon. Their contract had six more years to run. There had been some talk of his going back to an Earth University when he was nineteen, which would be a year before their return. He had never thought of going down earlier. But neither, so far as he knew, had Paul.

His mother was in the apartment when he arrived. She did a job of work outside the family, as everyone in the Bubble did, but her duties in the Food Programming Section were geared to fit in with Marty's school day. She looked tired — more so than usual. She smiled and kissed him, and asked him how school had been. He wondered if she would say something about Paul — news travelled almost instantaneously around the Bubble — but she did not. Because of that, he said nothing either. They talked about ancient Rome; she said it had been her favourite period of History when she was a girl.

He asked her: "Did you ever get to visit there? Rome, I mean?"

She nodded. "We spent a year there once. Father — your grandfather — had lived there when he was an art student."

"What's it like?"

"Oh, well . . ." She looked at him. "You've seen modern Rome on the films. That one last week."

"I know. But I mean — what's it really like?"

She looked away from him. "It's so long ago, Marty. I don't remember properly." She looked through the window towards the ramp. "I think that's your father."

Marty glanced at his finger-watch. "It's too early for him."

"He said he might get away early today." The door opened, and she said with what sounded like relief: "Hello, darling."

They kissed, and his father said: "Hi, boy. They let me off the leash half an hour before time. How about you and me heading up to the reservoir and catching us two or three trout for supper?"


The reservoir, like the park in which it stood, was one of the things intended to make life more natural. Keeping the recirculated water of the Bubble in this small open lake meant an extra cost in filtering and purifying plant. All such costs had to be very carefully considered. The Moon colony did what it could towards paying its way by mining and refining precious metals which were rocketed back to the mother planet, but apart from that its value lay in the less commercial fields of astronomical, selenographic and interplanetary research. The tax payers back home footed the bill, and there was small scope for luxuries. This one, though, was regarded as justifiable. The water in the lake was only a degree or so below the Bubble atmospheric temperature of eighteen degrees Centigrade, and trout flourished in it. Anyone who wanted to fish for natural protein was at liberty to do so. Other fish were grown in tanks. Meat came from the factory farm, with battery chicken as the mainstay.

Marty and his father made their way through the park to their usual fishing spot. There were four carefully trimmed lawns, flower beds and borders, a clump of shrubbery. Everything was calculated for economy and for the carefully planned balance of life in the Bubble. The flowers were specially bred to last and all the shrubs were evergreens: deciduous plants could have been trained to adapt to a world with no seasons, but their falling leaves would have been a nuisance.

The lake had been constructed asymmetrically, in a distorted kidney shape. The Bubble itself had to be a regular hemisphere, but as far as possible things inside it were given irregular shapes and lines in an attempt to avoid monotony. Even so, even with a part of its rim left in the irregular black basalt of the Moon's natural surface, the pool could not seem anything but artificial. Anyway, there was not an inch of its border, of any place inside the Bubble, that was not as familiar to Marty as the walls of his bedroom. Nothing changed. Changing things would have cost money.

They fished in silence for a time. During lunar night the Bubble was artificially lit by high-poled lamps which were faded out towards the end of the twelve-hour day through a rheostat at the electricity plant. At the moment they were still fully lit. Marty could see the others fishing round them, twenty or thirty, each in the place to which he came automatically. He thought of a feature film he had seen on TV about salmon fishing in Norway, with a thigh-booted man standing out in a torrent that foamed round his legs, and the valley empty to the distant grey horizon.

His father said: "You heard about Paul."

It was not a question. He nodded.

"Yes, he told me."

"I was talking to his father today. There's a medical factor involved. You know what a long streak Paul has turned into. They've always known that rehabilitation to Earth gravity is tougher on tall Lunarites — it's pretty obvious why — and recently they've come to the view that if you leave things too late you get permanent posture trouble. The doctors think Paul's that sort of case."

"I see."

"The Millers aren't happy about it, but they have to put his health first of course. They've only got three years of contract to run, but it's a long time."

Marty asked: "Where will he be living, on Earth?"

"With his grandparents in California. Just outside San Francisco."

"Sounds like a good place. We've been doing the United States in geography."

"Pretty good. I'm from New England myself."

Marty knew that, and also knew it was something his parents did not normally talk about. In the Bubble there was a good deal of general talk about Earth — about what TV showed was happening there — but people did not speak much about their own earlier lives.

After a pause, his father said again: "The Millers have only three years to go themselves. That helps."

"I suppose it does."

His father cast, and the line floated out across the placid unrippled waters. He said:

"Fifty generations of fish that have never seen a real fly but they still rise to the lure. This is a tricky problem, Marty. I've not talked about it before because it's just about impossible to explain it. Some people send their children down when they're four or five. That means they grow up as strangers, with strangers. There's a case for it. You can make a case for doing it at any age. The Dickinsons sent Clive when he was twelve because that was the age for entry to Peter Dickinson's old boarding school in England.

"We gave it a lot of thought, your mother and I. We decided to keep you till you were ready for University. Maybe we were being selfish — I don't know. One of the arguments on our side was that you and Paul were such buddies — had been since you crawled round a sandpit together, before you could walk. I guess that one has kind of blown up in our faces."

Marty did not say anything. His father went on:

"We've been thinking about things again. We decided you are old enough to make a decision for yourself. If you want to go down, we'll fix it."

"Where would I live?"

"We've got relatives in different places. You could have a choice."

His father had spoken evenly and casually, but Marty realized there was nothing casual about this, nor about the decision he should make. He was excited, and guessed the excitement could have shown in his voice. He was a bit ashamed and, realizing that, realized something else — that it really would mean leaving them, for six long years. He would be down on Earth and they would be still up here in the Bubble. He imagined seeing his mother's anxious face, not in reality but on the flickering circle of the visiphone screen, rationed to a few minutes at a time. He said quickly:

"It doesn't matter. I don't want to go down."

"You're sure of that? You could give it thought. You don't have to make up your mind right away."

"I'm sure," he said. "I'm fine here."

"Then I'm very glad. Especially on account of your mother. She made me promise not to say this before you decided, but she's not well." He caught Marty's quick look, and went on: "No, it's not anything serious. It's just that life here is more of a strain on some people than others. They miss things more, things they knew back on Earth. Your mother does."

But you don't, Marty thought with sudden resentment. He looked at his father's tall upright figure, the strong chin, high-cheekboned face, steady grey eyes. You're happy enough here.

"It would have been rough for her if you had decided to go. It's going to be pretty rough for Mrs Miller."

The excitement had gone; in its place there was a sick feeling in his stomach. He had been offered the trip to Earth and had turned it down. There was no going back — he was stuck with the Bubble now.

His father said: "Hey, you're not watching your line! That looks like a big one."

He went with the Millers by crawler to the launch station. It was six miles away along the edge of the Sea of Rains, as a precaution against blow-ups damaging or maybe even destroying the Bubble. The caterpillar tracks took them steadily with occasional jolts across the Moon's surface, from time to time plunging through dust pockets and sending dust scattering on either side, a shower of floating sparks in the rays of the risen sun.

Nobody spoke much. At the launch station they went on board with Paul and saw him for the last time, with all of them crowded together in the capsule. There was the bunk in which he would lie, cushioned for take-off. And for landing. It was hard to believe that in a few weeks he would be breathing the air of Earth, not inside a protective dome but out of the whole wide sky of the planet.

Paul said: "You'll write to me. I'm counting on that."

"Sure," Marty said. "You, too. If you don't find you have too many other things to do."

But he would, of course. Paul said:

"I won't. Bye, Mum, Dad. I'll visiphone you right away, soon as I land."

Mrs Miller kissed Paul. Mr Miller put a hand on his shoulder, squeezing hard. Then they had to get out and take a cabin across to the control centre. From the viewing level

they heard the relay of the count-down, and saw the exhaust gases rise in a fiery cloud from the pit before the ship itself began to rise, sliding out of its sheath, slowly at first and then faster and faster until it was a gleaming vanishing speck in the sky. That was when Mrs Miller started crying.

She had stopped by the time they took the crawler back to the Bubble, but the silence was worse that on the way out. Marty left them at the main airlock to make his way home. Mr Miller said:

"Thanks for coming along, Marty."

Mrs Miller said: "You'll come and see us still?" Her hands held his lightly. "We wouldn't like to lose touch with you, Marty."

As if one could lose touch with anyone inside the confines of the Bubble. He said:

"I won't lose touch, Mrs Miller."

*Written by John Christopher*
*Illustrated by Peter Foster*

# LETTERS FROM A

Pat Edwards

GTS: MS 198-7632-5BZ4-809
ARCARPOUS INSTRUCTIONAL UNIT NO 1769

TO: E1624-2167-921.084     SUNNYVALE PS 129370

INFO NEEDED RE LIFE STYLE ON YR PLANET.    PART OF CURRENT SOCIAL
SCIENCE RESEARCH PROJECT.    BUT CANNOT BELIEVE U CLD HVE ANYTHING THAT
WLD BE INTERESTING. ACCORDING TO MY TEXT BKS EARTH IS VERY PRIMITIVE.
HAD HOPED TO BE ALLOCATED ZOTL OR EUXYL OR ONE OF NEWLY DISCOVERED
PLANETS, BUT WAS SENT TO WORK ON STIMULATOR DURING PROJECT ALLOCATION
BECAUSE MY MOOD INDICATED SEVERE BOREDOM.   AM STUCK WITH EARTH AND U.
PLS SEND ANSWERS TO FLWG QUESTIONS BY GALACTIC TELEXIAL FLASH,
CHANNEL ARC 56-219-TSY-669.

1     YR AGE AND SEX
2     YR RATING IN THE EDUCATIONAL HIERACHY
3     YR CAREER SLOT
4     YR DIET PREFERENCES AND INTERESTS

FURTHER QUESTIONS WILL FOLLOW.

SIGNED: T1874.93X


MS 198-7632-5BZ4-810
ARCARPOUS INSTRUCTIONAL UNIT NO 1769

TO: E1624-2167-921.084     SUNNYVALE PS 129370

DON'T LIKE TONE OF YR MESSAGE.   INFO NEEDED FOR ROUTINE INTER-
GALACTIC INSTRUCTIONAL UNIT PROJECT. DON'T U HVE PROJECTS ON EARTH?
CAN ONLY PRESUME YR IGNORANCE PROVES EARTH REALLY IS PRIMITIVE DUMP
I'VE ALWAYS HEARD IT IS.
PLS FLASH REPLY IMMED.

SIGNED: T1874.93X

# DISTANT PLANET

GTS: MS 198-7632-5BZ4-811
ARCARPOUS INSTRUCTIONAL UNIT NO 1769

TO: E1624-2167-921.084:   SUNNYVALE PS 129370

OH, ALL RIGHT.  MY ASSIGNMENT IS TO PROFILE PERSON FR ANOTHER PLANET
FOR PURPOSES OF COMPARISON WITH OWN LIFE ON ARCARPOUS AND TO EXTEND
MY KNOWLEDGE OF UNIVERSE.  I WILL BE PRESENTING INFO AS A
VISUO-KINETIC CHART, USNG SOLAR COLOUR AND FISTEXLY PRINT.

HVE NOTED THAT THE WORD PROJECT IS FAMILIAR TO U.  PLS FLASH REPLY
IMMED.

SIGNED: T1874.93X

..32-5BZ4-812
.- INSTRUCTIONAL UNIT NO 1769

TO: LIZ HARNETT, E1624-2167-921.084   SUNNYVALE PS 129370

THK U FOR INFO.  I TOO AM AGED 12 AND FEMALE.  SOME QUERIES:  WHY NO
EDUCATIONAL RATING?  SURELY ALL EARTHERS ARE RATED AT BIRTH FOR
LEARNING CLASSIFICATION?  WHAT DOES 'BEING AROUND THE MIDDLE OF THE
CLASS' MEAN?  IT IS UNFAMILIAR TERM TO ME.  ALSO, HOW CAN YR SOCIETY
FUNCTION EFFICIENTLY WHEN ITS MEMBERS DO NOT KNOW EXACTLY WHAT TASKS
THEY WILL DO AT END OF TRAINING?  SURELY GIVING UNFORMED INDIVIDUALS
FREE CHOICE OF LIFE TASKS CAN ONLY LEAD TO CHAOS AND DISASTER?

PLS DEFINE HAMBURGERS, FISH N CHIPS, COKE, KENTUCKY FRIED, VEGEMITE.
ALL ARE UNFAMILIAR.

HVE CHECKED WITH MY INSTRUCTOR AND FIND TV IS OBSOLETE TERM FOR
PICTOAUDIOSCOPE.  WHY DO U CHOOSE TO WATCH AN EDUCATIONAL MEDIUM IN
LEISURE TIME?  ALSO WHAT DOES SURFING MEAN?

SIGNED:  YANDLOTUR T1874.93X

GTS: MS 198-7632-5BZ4-813
ARCARPOUS INSTRUCTIONAL UNIT NO 1769

TO: LIZ E1624-2167-921.084   SUNNYVALE PS 129370

WHY ADDRESS ME AS YANDI?   HERE ON ARCARPOUS ONLY FULL NAMES OR
NUMBERS ARE USED.   BUT DID NOT FIND IT DISPLEASING.   I FIND IT HARD
TO BELIEVE FREEDOM U DESCRIBE.   YR INSTRUCTIONAL UNIT SOUNDS
FRIGHTENINGLY RELAXED.   IMPOSS. TO IMAGINE YR TRAINING.   CAN U REALLY
COME TOP OF YR CLASS IF U DECIDE TO WORK HARD?   WON'T THIS UPSET THE
COMPUTERSTATS FOR YR AREA?   ALSO DIFFICULT TO GRASP THAT U REALLY CAN
CHOOSE YR LIFE TASK.   I HVE ALWAYS KNOWN I AM TO BE A COMPUTALLY
ASSISTANT AND WORK IN THE INTER-GALACTIC TRADE CENTRE, LEVEL 5926.
WE ARE NOT ENCOURAGED TO ASK HOW WE ARE SORTED INTO OUR CAREER SLOTS.
YR WAY SOUNDS MUCH MORE EXCITING.

NO ONE I KNOW HAS EVER HEARD OF YR DIET FAVOURITES.   MINE ARE ZENOBIC
STEAKS, MIROFLAX BERRIES AND FROZEN XYLTP MILK SWEET, WHICH IS
WHIPPED AND SERVED IN CONICAL-SHAPED PANCAKES.   WE CALL IT GALACTIC
SNOW.   EVER HEARD OF IT?

QUERY:   WHAT STORIES DO U WATCH ON YR TV AND HOW DOES SURF RELATE TO
WATER?

SIGNED:   YANDLOTUR T1874.93X

---

GTS: MS 198-17632-5BZ4-814
ARCARPOUS INSTRUCTIONAL UNIT NO 1769

DEAR LIZ: E1624-2167-921.084   SUNNYVALE PS 129370

HVE RELUCTANTLY DECIDED THAT EARTH IS FAR FR THE BACKWARD PLANET I
WAS LED TO BELIEVE.   ARE ALL YR YEAR-MATES LIKE U?   HVE U BEEN
TALKING ABOUT OUR COMMUNICATIONS TO YR BEDSTERS EACH NIGHT?   MINE ARE
AS FASCINATED AS I BY YR STRANGE AND WONDERFUL LIFE-STYLE.

ZENOBIC STEAKS COME FR ZENOBS, EIGHT-LEGGED MAMMALS BRED IN OUR
MOUNTAIN REGIONS.   THEY ARE BEST COOKED WELL, THEN SMOTHERED WITH
PECKSIE NUTS.   MIROFLAX FRUIT IS GREEN AND VERY SWEET.   THE BUSHES
ARE CULTIVATED IN GR 3 DESERTS.   YR ICE-CREAM DOES SOUND LIKE OUR
GALACTIC SNOW.   THE XYLTO IS A SMALL DOMESTIC ANIMAL THAT PRODUCES A
PURPLE FLUID WE CALL MILK.   WHAT IS A COW?   WISH WE HAD MOVIES AND
SERIALS TO WATCH LIKE U.   THK U FOR DESCRIBING SURF.   HAD READ ABOUT
SEAS.   BUT DID NOT REALISE THE TWO WENT TOGETHER.   MOST NEW PLANETS
LIKE ARCARPOUS HVE TO CREATE WATER ARTIFICALLY.   THERE ARE NO OCEANS
OR BEACHES.

SIGNED:   YANDI T1874.93X

GTS: MS 198-7632-5BZ4-815
ARCARPOUS INSTRUCTIONAL UNIT NO 1769

DEAR LIZ: E164-2167-921.084   SUNNYVALE PS 129370

THK U, THK U, THK U FOR THOSE HOLOGRAHIC FLICS.  WE SMUGGLED THEM
INTO OUR DORMA-UNIT LAST NIGHT AND VIEWED THEM OVER AND OVER AGAIN.
IT WAS WONDERFUL TO SEE WHAT U LOOKED LIKE.  I DID NOT FIND IT
IT FRIGHTENING.

TO ANSWER YR QUERY:  ONE'S YEAR-MATES ARE  ALL THOSE BORN IN SAME
YEAR IN A PARTICULAR AREA.  WE DO EVERYTHING TOGETHER UNTIL MATURITY,
BUT ARE DIVIDED INTO GROUPS OF 93 FOR INSTRUCTION AND REST PERIODS
(YOU'LL HVE NOTED I AM ALMOST AT BOTTOM OF MY GROUP BEING 93X).
BEDSTERS ARE THE PEOPLE WHO SLEEP EITHER SIDE OF U.  ONE USUALLY
BONDS CLOSEST WITH THEM.

MY TURN TO QUERY:  WHAT IS A MOTHER AND FATHER?

SIGNED:  YANDI T1874.93X

---

ARCARPOUS INSTRUCTIONAL UNIT NO 1769
.-76-7632-5BZ4-816

DEAREST LIZ:  E1624-2167-921.084     SUNNYVALE PS 129370

THIS IS MY LAST COMUNICATION.  MY INSTRUCTOR HAS ORDERED TELEXIAL
CABLE TO BE CLEARED AND OUR PROJECTS COMPLETED.  NEXT INSTRUCTIONAL
UNIT PROJECT IS ABOUT THE DEVELOPMENT OF TRIAMPUTER MATHEMATICS.
ALREADY CAN FEEL MY MOOD MONITOR SWNGING TO 'SEVERE BOREDOM'.

FORGOT TO TELL U ABOUT MOOD MONITORS.  THEY ARE STRAPPED TO OUR
FOREHEADS AND OUR INSTRUCTORS CHECK THEM EVERY HOUR SO THEY CAN VARY
OUR TASKS OR CHIDE US ACCORDING TO WHAT THEY THINK IS PROPER.

WHEN I READ YR DESCRIPTION OF A MOTHER AND FATHER I HAD WATER IN MY
EYES.  I THOUGHT I WAS MALFUNCTIONING, BUT A CHECK IN THE WORDPUTER
TOLD ME THIS ABNORMALITY IS CAUSED BY SADNESS.  FOR FIRST TIME MY
MOOD MONITOR TURNED DEEP BLUE.

BEFORE I SIGN OFF I WANT TO ENTRUST U WITH A SECRET.  WHEN I REACH
MATURITY I PLAN TO STOWAWAY ON A GALACTIC TRADER AND HITCH A RIDE TO
EARTH.  IT SOUNDS LIKE MYTHICAL HEAVEN I READ OF ONCE IN AN OLD, OLD
CONDENSOGRAH.  PLS WATCH FOR ME IN FIVE OR SIX YRS TIME.

SIGNED:  YOUR ENVIOUS AND OH-SO-SAD FRIEND

YANDI

PS:  YOU'LL HVE NO TROUBLE RECOGNISING ME.  ALL ARCARPOUSIANS HVE
MULTI-FACETED EYES AND SIX LIMBS.

# CONTACT WITH AN

# Alien!

The three space children, Lira, Peaty and Rex, are on the school space bus travelling back to their home planets from Velos at the end of school term.

When they find that they are the only three left aboard, they can't resist experimenting with the controls. No pilots drive these buses, they are operated by a computer. They knew they weren't supposed to play with the controls — but they had. Now, out of control, they are blasting away from their home galaxy, towards the unknown.

Frightened and tired, there seems nothing else they can do but climb onto the air beds and try to rest . . .

**T**he children were fast asleep when the space bus left the Velos galaxy and shot out into the black starless universe.

Lira grew agitated and restless toward morning. She started tossing, turning and muttering, then awoke with a start and lay quietly with her eyes closed, recalling a fearful dream. She let the recollection of the mess they were in flood back to her.

"You are in trouble, aren't you?" a voice said. She opened her eyes and looked around, but the boys were still fast asleep.

"Who said that?" she thought. "Am I hearing things?"

"No, you're not. It's me."

Lira sat up and looked around, "Where are you?" she asked, but there was only silence. *I'm going off my head*, she thought sadly.

"Now, don't be silly! You sound perfectly sane to me."

Lira frowned and rolled over. She covered her ears with her hands and whimpered.

"Don't be afraid," said the voice. "You're only a young one of the species, aren't you? And you're lost."

"Yes," Lira thought, "and I'm scared."

"There's no need to be scared. I'm out here, too, and I'm not scared."

**L**ira jumped up and looked around. "Where are you, then?" she asked loudly.

Her voice echoed in the silence and the boys awoke with a start.

"I'm not in your ship. I'm . . ."

The voice faded with the boys' interference.

"Lira! What's the matter?" They looked into her frightened face.

"Ssshh Listen!" They listened, but the voice had gone.

"I thought I heard someone talking to me," said Lira weakly. Rex and Peaty glanced at each other. Rex smoothed her damp brow. "Try to rest. It was probably a nightmare."

"Was it just a dream?" Lira thought in agitation.

"No, it wasn't a dream," the voice said. "You must not block me out like that. If you listen, I'll explain."

**S**he clutched at the boys. "Did you hear that? Did you hear the voice? It said I have to listen!"

They shook their heads. "Peaty, get Lira some water," Rex said quickly. "I think she's sick."

"Am I sick?" Lira frowned. "I don't feel sick."

Peaty came back with a bubble of water and she drank it obediently.

"Lie down and relax," Rex said soothingly. "You might feel better in a little while." He helped her lie down again and beckoned Peaty away from her.

"It's probably the strain we're under. We don't know her very well. She may not be as tough as she makes out. If we just leave her alone, she'll probably be all right."

Lira nestled into the air bed. "You're not sick," the voice said. "Just relax and listen to me."

"All right," she thought, "I'll relax. Who are you and where are you and how are you talking to me?"

"Oh," the voice said. "So many questions from one so young! First I'll tell you that I'm touching your mind and when you use your mouth to talk, it blocks me out. No, wait! Don't start thinking like that, it's all babble to me. I can only receive clear thought." Lira stopped the turmoil in her mind with an effort.

"Thank you," the voice said. "Now, think of one part of your brain as a small pocket communicator, like that one you carry on your utility belt. You press a button to send and release it to receive. Think of your mind as the communicator and we'll have proper contact. All right, try to send."

Lira pretended she was pushing a mental button.

"Who are you?" she asked loudly and released the button.

There were long seconds of silence. She felt pain sear through her head, her face screwed tight and her hands blocked her ears.

"Oh, child," the voice gasped. "The pain will go. Wait for me."

The voice went, and so did the pain.

Lira lay waiting, gazing at the ceiling of the bus and at the distant galaxy through the window.

"I'm sorry child." The voice came back. "I wasn't prepared for such a high power blast. The pain you felt was feedback of my pain. I picked up your distress whispers and had to tune almost to full to receive and send. I thought that was the limit of your power but it appears I was greatly mistaken. I now see that you are an extremely gifted and powerful child. You must mentally tune your volume to extreme low, or if you can't understand that, endeavour to whisper your thoughts. Another blast like the first could quite possibly damage me and destroy hope for both of us. Now I shall open to receive and you may send, but, remember, be as gentle as you can."

Lira nodded to the space bus ceiling and thought, "Who are you and where are you?"

"Very good, child. Perhaps you would count for me, increasing volume at each number. I have control over my receiver and can adjust down to achieve normal levels for both of us. When I stop, you lock onto that volume and we will be comfortable."

Lira started counting.

"Stop! Stop, child! oh dear, you certainly are powerful. Three! That will have to do. Is your level comfortable?"

"I'll get used to it," Lira said quietly. "Now, will you please tell me who you are and where you are?"

"Of course, child. My name is Radar II and I am in a small craft almost directly ahead of your ship. With your increased speed, you should have a visual contact with me in a few minutes."

"Can you help us?" Lira asked with rising excitement.

"No, my dear, I'm afraid I can't," the voice said sadly. "You see, I'm lost too. I have been for some time, and I'm afraid my life support system will give out in a matter of days. I was wondering if you could pick me up."

Lira's heart fell to her boots.

"Of course we can. We'll try, anyway. None of us knows how to work the ship properly, but we'll try."

"Thank you, child."

She felt relief sing through her. "Was that you I felt?" she asked.

"Yes," the voice said. "This telepathic form of communication carries emotions more easily than specific word patterns, but there isn't time for that now. You must stop your ship almost immediately if I am to be retrieved."

Lira jumped up.

"You'll have to be quiet while I talk to the boys, but I'll leave myself open for you."

She looked around for the boys, "Rex! Peaty!" she called. "We have to stop the ship. There's somebody out there and he wants us to pick him up!"

The boys were sitting at the flight control panel and she ran to them.

"Quickly! Stop the ship, otherwise we'll pass him and his life support has only two days left."

They stared at her aghast. Peaty got up and backed away. "She's gone mad!" he gasped.

"**I** haven't gone mad! It's the voice I was hearing. I've been talking to it, and I said we'd try to help."

"Poor Lira," Rex said softly. "Wouldn't you like to come and lie down?"

"No!" Lira cut him off. "I'm not mad! His name is Radar II and he's lost, like us! Please, Rex, please stop the bus, just for a minute. I'm not mad, really I'm not!"

"I know you're not mad, Lira," Rex said gently, "you're just a bit distraught. We all are." He put his arm around her and tried to lead her back to the air bed.

She looked out the window, desperately trying to see the small craft that should have been coming into view.

"Wait! The microwave scanner. Have a look on the scanner. Computer!" she cried, "switch off automatic evasive. We're probably going around him now. Look at the screen, Rex. Just look!" she pleaded.

"Evasive off," the computer droned.

Rex went over to activate the scanner.

He stared, then jumped. "Peaty, she's right! There is something out there. Come and look!"

"We might be able to see from the window!" Lira rushed to the side of the ship and looked out. "There! We're passing him, Rex."

She watched the tiny craft being left behind. "He's gone," she said sadly. "We've lost him."

"No, not yet." Rex strapped himself at the controls. "Give me a hand, Peaty!"

Lira was afraid to make contact with Radar II in case she communicated her fear to him. She hung onto the window, staring hard at the almost invisible craft.

"Lira, strap in at the scanner. We'll need you to guide us. Hang on," Rex called and fired the forward jets.

Lira slipped off her feet and slid along the floor. Rex cut the jets. "Strap in, Lira, quick!"

She scrambled to the seat and dragged herself into it. "Fire again," Rex ordered Peaty.

He left the jets on for a little longer this time before cutting them. Each time he fired the bus slowed until after three more blasts it had stopped.

Rex smiled across at Lira. "Sorry about the first part. I had no idea the brakes were so good. I jammed them on a bit too hard."

"Well, we've stopped," Lira laughed. "That's all I care about."

"Right. Where is your friend?"

66

**D**own here. He's nearly off the edge of the screen, but he's coming in our direction," said Lira.

"Good," Rex said. "Peaty and I will work the controls and you'll have to direct us. We don't know anything about those points and degrees, so you'll just have to say left or right or whatever it is. I'm going to fire the forward jets to back us up to him."

"Why didn't you use them before?" Peaty burst out. "We could have backed up to my planet."

"By the time I thought of it there was nowhere to back up to," said Rex sadly.

Peaty stared dismally out the window and Lira leaned over and touched his shoulder. "It's all right, Peaty, we'll get home. This person we're going to pick up may be able to help us." She looked back down and concentrated on directing Rex.

"Visual contact," Radar II said. Lira jumped and the boys turned to look at her.

"I'm sorry," said Radar II. "I startled you. I didn't hear from you for so long, and when you went past me and disappeared out of sight, I gave up hope."

"We nearly did lose you," Lira smiled. "The boys wouldn't believe me. They thought I'd gone mad."

"Are you all right, Lira?" Rex asked.

"Oh yes," Lira glanced up. "I'm talking to Radar II."

"Are you, really?" Peaty asked.

"Yes, I am," she said indignantly, "and you've interrupted us".

"If you really are talking to him," Rex said, "ask him if he has any control over his ship and if he does, how much".

Lira nodded and opened communication with Radar II again.

"If we're going to pick this Radar person up, Peaty," Rex said, "we'll have to find out if this bus has airlocks and some sort of docking device. Why don't you switch the computer off vocal and fiddle around with it, to see what you can come up with?"

Peaty nodded. "I'm sick of the sound of that voice, anyway," he said.

"Radar II says he hasn't much control of his ship at all. He knows how to get in and out and work the food machine, but otherwise he just sits there and plays with his consol and his toes," Lira frowned.

"Plays with his toes! How strange." Rex lapsed into a thoughtful silence.

"We've got an airlock on the other side of the exit chute," Peaty called, "and a magnetic locking device on top of the rear stabiliser."

**G**reat," Rex grinned. "Now all we have to do is get close enough to pull him in. That's if there's a magnetic sensor in his ship."

"It's not a ship," Lira said slowly. "It's only a small craft and, yes, he says he probably has one of those things. They would have put one in for his retrieval."

"All right," Rex said. "How close are we?"

Lira looked at the screen. "Nearly there."

"Peaty, get the computer ready to activate the field, and when I give the word, punch it in. I'm going to try coming up underneath him. Lira, you'll have to watch him from the window and direct me." He looked at her in admiration. "You really can talk to him, can't you?" Lira smiled.

Docking Radar II was much more difficult than any of them had suspected. With Lira running up and down the side windows shouting directions and two complete misses, it took nearly three galactic hours before they finally locked the little craft in.

When it was done Rex slumped into his chair exhausted. "Now all we've got to do is get him inside," he said.

"I'll go," Peaty offered.

"No," Rex swivelled his chair around. "You'll have to work the airlock. Besides, you don't know anything about floating. I'd better go."

"No!" Lira stopped him. "I'll go. I found him and I can talk to him. It'll be much better if I go."

"Why can't he come in by himself?" Rex asked her.

They watched Lira stop and put her hand up to keep them quiet while she communicated.

"He says he would rather someone helped him. He says he apologises for the trouble he's put us to but he's never been in and out of spacecrafts without someone there to help him."

"He doesn't sound very bright." Peaty pulled a face.

"He's all right!" Lira burst out. "He's an adult, and I don't mind going to get him at all."

"I was wondering about the magnetic sensitisers in our belts," Rex said. "Do you think they'll lock onto the landing bay lock?"

"I expect so. If yours pulled you into the chair, I don't see why it won't pull me onto the docking stabiliser," Lira said.

"What about asking the computer, Peaty? There might be a difference between the two fields."

Peaty turned to the computer and tapped at the keys. "No, you're right, Rex," he said. "It's negative."

"Good! Come on then, Lira. I'll put you into the airlock," said Rex.

**L**ira touched a button on her wrist to activate her space field before she stepped into the airlock. The crackling little blue lights covered her entirely and formed a small aura around her face.

"It's working all right Rex," she nodded, her voice sounding slightly muffled through the field. She stepped into the airlock, pulled the end of a cord out of her belt and clipped it to a ring inside the lock.

Rex called to Peaty who closed the airlock and Lira floated out and onto the stabiliser.

"I'm coming up to your door now," she thought to Radar II. "Are you ready?"

"Of course I'm ready. I won't suffocate out there, will I?"

"Huh," Lira thought. "You're wearing your suit, aren't you?"

"Of course I am, child."

"Then switch on your space field and get into the airlock."

"My dear, I haven't the faintest idea what you're talking about."

"Are there little coloured dots around your cuffs?"

"Yes, but I've had specific instructions not to touch or to attempt to play with them unless given the order. Dear child, your astonishment is quite clear. I assure you that I will explain myself fully at the earliest opportunity."

"There's a red button on the side of your right wrist. Press it and it will activate the space field. Haven't you ever had a field on before?" Lira asked, a little impatiently.

"Why, goodness me, no! I've never been into space before. Now what are your instructions about the airlock?"

"Airlock? But you said you know how it works."

"I do, but I cannot use it unless specifically ordered."

"I see. Well, get into the airlock and close the door."

"Now what?"

"I don't know," Lira said. "I don't know how your locks works. Ours is controlled by the computer."

"Is it? Mine is controlled by these two coloured buttons. One is red and one is green. The red button is alight now, and if I push the green one they will both become green and the outer door will open."

"Why haven't you pushed it, then?"

"I am waiting for your instructions, child."

Lira was inclined to agree with Peaty that Radar II did not sound very intelligent.

"All right," she said. "Push the green button."

**S**he waited for the door to open, wondering whether she should shake his hand or introduce herself.

"Completely unnecessary, child. I'm here," he said, and tried to amble the few paces across the flight stabiliser.

Lira stared at him and jumped backwards in fear.

"What! What *are* you?"

He was floating away from the stabiliser and started to kick and squirm awkwardly.

"I won't be anything soon, unless you take hold of me. I think I am being swept away by this strange wind."

Lira jumped and wrapped her arms around the ugly little man. They sailed to the end of her safety line and stopped.

"Thank you very much," he said, and his mouth didn't move.

"I'm sorry," Lira stuttered. "You scared me."

"Never mind that now. What about taking me inside your ship? I shall loop my arms around your neck like this. I'm very good at hanging on that way and you can pull us in."

She touched a button on the safety line box and it started to wind them in. "Well, fancy that," the ugly little man said when he saw what was happening.

When they got up to the airlock, Lira stopped.

"I'm not taking you any further unless you tell me what you are and where you come from. For all I know you might be a dangerous form of life from a galaxy we haven't discovered yet. You certainly don't look human to me, and if you are, you're the ugliest little man I've ever met." She said it at her normal talking volume and saw it was hurting him, but she was becoming angry.

His large wide mouth curled back and he bared his fangs.

"You're a cruel human child and I shall bite you if you do that again! Not only is it dangerous but it is extremely painful."

"I won't do it again if you tell me what you are and where you come from." Lira controlled her urge to scream at him.

"My dear child, of course I'm not human; whatever led you to that idea? I am a chimpanzee and I come from the planet Earth, which is situated on the edge of a galaxy called the Milky Way."

*Text by Jenny Summerville*
*Illustrated by Peter Foster*

# ANIMALNAUTS

**Next time people are talking about our brave astronauts, spare a thought for the real, first travellers in space.**

Not counting the fruit flies, sea urchin eggs, and unnamed cats, mice and rabbits, the list goes like this:

1  *1948*  Albert, male monkey, dies aloft in a US rocket.

2  *1949–1959*  Several dogs, rabbits, and cats are sent up in USSR V–24 and V–54 rockets. Only the dogs wear space suits. All die.

3  *1951*  One unnamed monkey and several nameless mice die in US Aerobee rocket.

4  *1952*  Rhesus monkeys, Pat and Mike, in a US Aerobee rocket, become first animalnauts to enter — and die in — the upper atmosphere.

5  *3 Nov 1957*  Laika, female Samoyed husky, becomes first animal to orbit the earth. She travels in a USSR Sputnik 2 satellite. She dies after ten days when her oxygen runs out.

6  *28 May 1959*  Able and Baker, two monkeys, become first animalnauts to be recovered from a missile flight in a US Jupiter rocket. Able dies a few days later while having an

... 4 Dec 1959 Sam, a monkey, is parachuted safely back to earth after rocketing to an altitude of 62.5 km in a US Little Joe rocket.

8 *Jan 1960* Miss Sam, another monkey flies for eight mins to an altitude of 13.5 km. She is reunited with Sam on board a US aircraft carrier. They exchange relieved hugs.

9 *19 Aug 1960* Belka and Strelka, female Samoyed huskies, complete just over seventeen orbits of the earth in twenty-five hours in a USSR Sputnik 5–Spacecraft 2, thus becoming the first animalnauts to be safely recovered from Orbit. Both later have several litters of normal puppies. One of Strelka's was given to USA President JF Kennedy.

10 *7 Dec 1960* Female Samoyeds, Ptsyolka and Mushka die when their capsule burns up on re-entry — spacecraft was USSR Sputnik 6–Spacecraft 3.

11 *31 Jan 1961* Ham, a male chimpanzee, completes sixteen and a half minutes suborbital flight in a US Mercury-Redstone 2 Spacecraft. Ham retired to Washington's National Zoological Park.

12 *1961* Enos, a male chimpanzee, completes first US orbital flight. (The experience didn't turn him off banana pellets. He went on happily eating them back down on earth.)

13 *9 Mar 1961* Female Samoyed, Chavnushka returns in good condition from an elliptical orbit in a USSR Sputnik 9–Spacecraft 4. It's recorded that she ate heartily during the voyage.

14 *25 Mar 1961* Another female Samoyed, Zvezdochka (Little Star) successfully completes seventeen orbits. She was given her name by Cosmonaut Yuri Gargarin, whose historic flight followed hers on 12 April 1961.

# IT'S A PLANE!
## IT'S A BIRD!
# It's Pegasus!

Who — or what — was Pegasus?

In the Greek myths, Pegasus was a beautiful white horse with huge wings. It is said that he sprang from a pool of blood spilt when Perseus chopped off the Medusa's head. As soon as he was born, Pegasus flew to Mount Helicon where the nine Muses lived. There he struck the ground with his front hoof and immediately a spring of clear water appeared. The spring was called 'Hippocrene' (which means the fountain of the horse) and its waters were thought to fill people with poetic inspiration.

News of Pegasus spread quickly though Greece and many people longed to ride this horse that could fly. One boy, Bellerophon, asked Athena, the goddess of wisdom, for help. Athena gave Bellerophon a magical golden bridle. As soon as he slipped the bridle over the horse's head, Bellerophon was able to command Pegasus to do whatever he asked.

They had many adventures together, including one in which they killed the Chimaera, a monster that was part-lion, part-goat and part-serpent. However, Bellerophon gradually began to think too much of himself, and in the end tried to

ride Pegasus to Olympus, the home of gods. Some versions of the story say that Pegasus refused, others say that Zeus sent a fly to sting the horse, but whatever it was, Bellerophon was thrown off and fell back to earth. He was made lame by the fall and wandered alone and homeless for the rest of his life. People believed he was cursed by the gods.

Pegasus went to live with Zeus in Olympus. When Zeus wanted to use his thunderbolt, Pegasus brought the thunder and lightning to him.

# SPACE TRAVELLERS

There was a witch, hump-backed and hooded,
Lived by herself in a burnt-out tree;
When storm winds shrieked and the moon was buried
And the dark of the forest was black as black,
She rose in the air like a rocket at sea,
>          Riding the wind,
>          Riding the night,
Riding the tempest to the moon and back.

There may be a man with a hump of silver,
Telescope eyes and a telephone ear,
Dials to twist and knobs to twiddle,
Waiting for a night when skies are clear,
To shoot from the scaffold with a blazing track,
>          Riding the dark,
>          Riding the cold,
Riding the silence to the moon and back.

*James Nimmo*

# Rocketing Thro

A time line showing the development of rockets from their invention up until the first moon landing.

**5 Oct. 1882**

American space-flight pioneer, Robert H. Goddard born. He will become known as the father of the modern rocket.

**1865**

Jules Verne's novel *From the Earth to the Moon* is published.

**1857**

Konstantin Edovardovich Ziolkovsky is born. He will become known as the father of space travel.

**1890**

German engineer, Hermann Ganswindt, makes the first modern proposal for a spaceship.

Rockets were invented by the Chinese around 1040. They used them to power arrows. Later, the Saracens introduced them to Europe and by the 15th century no European army was without its rocket corps. The pioneer of military rockets in Britain was William Congreve and he managed to improve the range and accuracy of these gunpowder rockets. Another English inventor, William Hale, devised ones that spun in flight and so kept stable. The British navy used rockets against the French at Boulonge in 1806 and against the Americans in 1814. But up till then they were thought of simply as weapons. Only the novelists dreamed of using rockets to escape up into space.

**From 1040 — 1857**

A rich French woman, Madame Clara Goquet gives the French Acadamy 100 000 francs which is to be given to the first man or men who succeed in establishing communication with another planet — but not with Mars!

Now a teacher, Ziolkovsky produces a paper that will establish him as a space pioneer. It describes the fundamental principles of rocket action as applied to escaping earth's gravity for flight in space.

Belgian, Dr André Bing takes out patent for all-important step principle for rockets.

Robert Goddard now a scientist, receives a patent in which liquid fuels for rocket propulsion are mentioned.

Robert Goddard demonstrates his recently invented anti-tank rocket to US army officials the day before the armistice. They are not impressed and it's regarded as only an interesting gadget until World War II. Actually it's the forerunner of the present Bazooka anti-tank weapon.

**16 Mar. 1926**

**Dec. 1900**

**1925**

**1903**

**1925**

**1911**

**1923**

**14 July 1914**

**1919**

**10 Nov. 1918**

**1928**

German engineer, Noordung presents modern design of a space station in the form of a w

Goddard flies world's first liquid-propellant rocket on Ward Farm near Auburn, Massachusetts. Local fire marshals are so alarmed they ban all future rocket experiments.

Germany's 'Society for Space Travel' formed. It's the world's first rocket society.

German engineer, Walter Hohmann writes a book analysing departure and return from the earth, free coasting in space and circumnavigation of other worlds.

German space-flight pioneer, Herman Oberth, devises a two-stage spaceship for a crew of two.

Goddard produces a booklet stating that it should be possible to use rocket-powered vehicles to send scientific instruments to the moon. Newspapers pile ridicule on him for suggesting such a fantastic thing.

**29 July 1969** — Neil Armstrong, aged 39, commander of Apollo XI, becomes first man to step on the moon.

**27 March 1968** — Yuri Gagarin killed in jet plane crash.

**23 April 1967** — Vladimir Mikhailovich Komarov, aged 40, becomes first man to die during space flight.

**3 June 1965** — Astronaut Edward H. White takes the first walk in space.

**16 June 1963** — 26-year-old, Valentina Vladimirovna Tereshkova becomes the first woman to orbit the earth.

**5 May 1961** — Alan B. Shepard, first US astronaut travels 453 km in a ballistic trajectory.

**12 April 1961** — Cosmonaut, Yuri Alekscyevich Gagarin, aged 27, becomes the first human to orbit the earth.

**14 Sept. 1959** — Space probe Lunik II strikes the moon. USSR and US develop intercontinental ballistic missiles.

**4 Oct. 1957** — Sputnik I goes into orbit around the earth.

**1 Jan. 1957** — International Geophysical year begins. Much is poured into rocket research. During the next 4 years, 55 satellites and space probes will be launched by the USA and the USSR.

**1946** — The German rocket research team, headed by Werner von Braun, crosses to the US.

**1945** — World War II ends and the German rocket research team surrenders to the Americans.

**1939-45** — During World War II the Germans invent a variety of rocket vehicles for the army. Some are solid-propellant, some are liquid-propellant. England, the US, Russia and Japan all develop smaller solid-propellant military rockets. The world-wide rocket industry has been born.

**July 1937** — German rocket research centre founded at Peenemünde. Here they finally produce the famous V2 long-range ballistic missile. It's the largest rocket vehicle to date.

**1933** — The world's 4th rocket society founded in Liverpool, England. It was called the "British Interplanetary Society".

**1932** — A group of "rocketeers" headed by 20-year-old Werner von Braun go to work for the German army.

**1930** — Charles Lindbergh (first man to fly solo across the Atlantic) comes to Goddard's aid and organises a small grant which allows Goddard to move to New Mexico. During the next 12 years the researcher will develop the first liquid-propellant rocket engine and the first gyro-controlled rocket guidance system. He will also develop rocket take-off units for US military aircraft.

**March 1930** — "American Interplanetary Society" — the world's 3rd rocket society is founded in New York. It later becomes the "American Rocket Society".

**1928** — World's 2nd rocket society, the "Austrian Society for High Altitude Exploration" is founded in Vienna.

**1928** — A French Prize for Astronautics is established. 5 000 francs is awarded for research... area...

81

# TRAVELLING IN SPACE

Feel like a quick trip in space?

Fine — you're on!

But first of all you've got to get a spacesuit (just in case you're planning to step outside) — and it has to be made just right.

*Here's a checklist*:

1  It has to have 11 layers of special materials.
2  One inner layer — the one that looks like long underwear, has to have around 90m of plastic tubing sewn into it. (That's so the water you'll be carrying in your primary life-support system or PLSS, can circulate and help keep you warm or cold according to what's needed.)
3  Another layer has to be filled with pressurised air and the seams must be heat sealed to make sure they are air tight.
4  Five of the outer layers need to be made of aluminised fabric to reflect dangerous rays of the sun away from your body and one of these must be specially designed to resist damage from micrometeoroids — those tiny, fast-moving particles of space dust that may hit you when you step outside your spacecraft.
5  The HUT or top part of the suit should be made of fibreglass and connect with the bubble-shaped helmet.

6 Gloves must have several layers. One layer should be dipped into a kind of plastic for extra strength and another specially designed to protect you from hot objects. Please see that the gloves have joints in the fingers and wrists so your hands can move freely.

7 Check to make sure that there are knee, ankle and elbow joints in your suit. It's embarrassing if you can't move.

8 Your PLSS should be made from a solid block of aluminium and be able to carry enough water and oxygen for a 7 hour space walk.

9 You'd be wise to practise moving around, because on earth your suit and PLSS will weigh around 113 kilograms. But don't worry, it will all weigh nothing in space.

10 Please take care of your suit. When you come back home again, it will be cleaned and retested — ready for your next mission!

*Now — what about your craft?*
If it's like the United States space shuttle, it will probably have 3 parts:

a the *orbiter* which is what you'll be in as you orbit earth.

b two *rocket boosters*: these will be separated from the orbiter by remote control after their fuel is used up. They'll float down by parachute and be picked up and taken back to base so they can be reused.

c the *external fuel tank* (or *ET*): this will pour fuel into the main engines of your orbiter until you reach a speed of *mach 26* (that's around 26 times the speed of sound). At that point the tank falls away from the orbiter or spacecraft and breaks up, most of the pieces changing to vapour. A new tank is needed for each flight.

*Okay — ready for lift-off?*
Buckle up and off you go. But please notice that you won't be sitting upright bravely grasping the controls, or waving to your fans out of a window. You'll be lying on your back, knees bent, feet braced against the wall. A little less glamorous than the way they do it in films or on TV shows, but a lot safer.

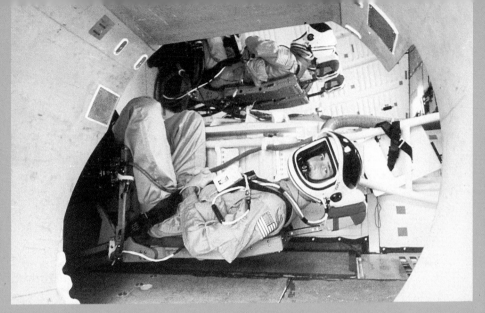

*A warning . . .*
You're not going to be your same old self up there, you know. At
lift-off your body will be three times as heavy during those moments
of escaping from earth's gravity. (The scientists call this 3G, by the
way.) But that will pass. In less than a minute, if your craft is the same
as the space shuttle, you'll be moving at the speed of sound (*mach
1*). A minute later and you'll be 50 km up and flying at *mach 4.5*.
Although you'll have broken the initial gravity tug, there's still enough
of a pull to keep you attached to the earth — which is just as well, or
you'd go flying off into deep space, and who knows where you'd end
up! This minor pull is called *microgravity* and it's what puts a
spacecraft into orbit.

Finally, here you are, 320 km high, spinning around the earth at more
than 28 000 kmh. (At that speed you could get from sea level to the
top of Mt Everest in one second. Imagine!)
    And how do you feel now? Taller? That's right. In microgravity you
can be up to 5 cm taller than you are on earth. Because you are now
weightless, your body is operating differently. For one thing, on earth
your blood is mostly in the lower part of your body, but now the blood
is spreading upwards so that your waist becomes smaller and your
face fuller. Oh yes — check your feet. They'll be narrower.
    But the main thing you'll notice is that you can't stand straight as
you do on earth. You'll be bending forward slightly at waist, hips and
knees. And unless you control them, your arms will float out in front
of you. As for your toes, well they'll insist on pointing, so that you
can't put your feet flat.
    By the way, you don't have to wear your cumbersome spacesuit

inside the cabin. That's just for strolling outside. Your flightsuit should be light, comfortable and fireproof.

But above all, it should have pockets all over it to hold the many small things you want to use — things like pens and pencils, notebooks, glasses, etc. If they aren't tucked safely into pockets they'll just float off. Fortunately, you'll find that there are strips of Velcro (you know, that material things stick to) all around the walls of the spacecraft. You can press a torch or comb or any small tool against these and they'll stay put until you need them.

*Feeling hungry? Wondering what you're going to eat?*

Well "what" isn't as much of a problem as "how". If you look at the picture you'll see that you'll need footstraps to hold you in place so you can use both hands to feed yourself. And you'll have to hold on to those utensils or lunch might just float off while you're not looking.

The menu could be almost as good as your favourite lunch on earth. We know that the US astronauts had hamburgers, chicken and noodles, scrambled eggs, soup, macaroni and cheese, peanut butter, applesauce, fruit, nuts, snacks and sweets. And to drink? Well, they had a choice of fruit juices and cordials, hot chocolate, coffee, tea or punch. No fizzy drinks, though. Why? Because they make you burp and that can be a real problem. Some astronauts have trouble keeping food down anyway when they're weightless. An unexpected burp could bring the whole meal up — total disaster in a small cabin!

By the way, only soft bread will be served, because no one wants crumbs floating around the place, and for the same reason, salt, pepper, sugar and mustard have to be liquid.

*What about a wash and brush up?*

First of all, banish any thoughts of a shower. All the time you're in space, you'll just have to be content with wiping your body with a damp face cloth and then towelling yourself dry.

A hand-washing device is good for a quick clean up because it keeps the water from floating around the cabin, but when you're finished, be sure to use your own towel. On space shuttles, each crew member has his or her own special coloured towels for the length of the trip.

When you use the toilet it's important to clip on a seat belt and to use the foot holders, otherwise it could be embarrassing. All liquid water from the wash bowl and toilet flows into a container which is dumped overboard as soon as it gets full. Solid wastes go into a separate container where they are dried up. They're taken back to earth and got rid of down here.

*And now for a sleep . . .*
Each bunk has a padded board for you to lie on. There's a sleeping bag, a curtain to pull across if you want some privacy and a reading light in case you fancy a quiet read. While you snooze, a sling or belt will keep you pressed gently against the board. As in an aeroplane, you'll have a mask to wear if the cabin light bothers you, and ear plugs to shut out noise . . .

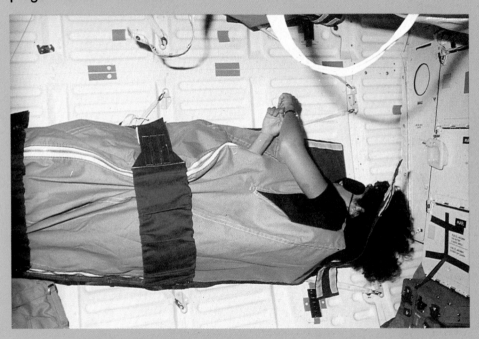

So, sleep well — and sweet dreams.
Oh yes, AND HAVE A NICE TRIP!

*Pat Edwards*

# A QUICK TRIP TO NOWHERE

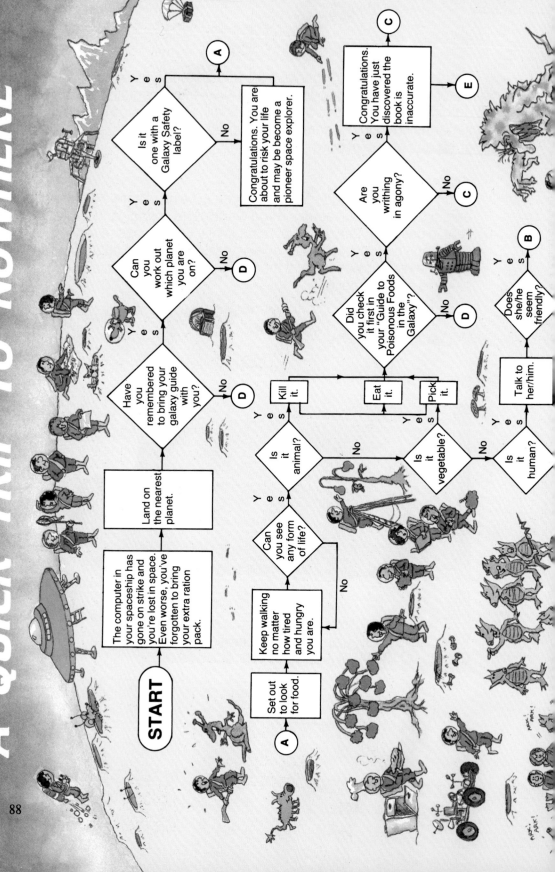

**START**

The computer in your spaceship has gone on strike and you're lost in space. Even worse, you've forgotten to bring your extra ration pack.

Land on the nearest planet.

Have you remembered to bring your galaxy guide with you? — **No** → D

**Yes**

Can you work out which planet you are on? — **No** → D

**Yes**

Is it one with a Galaxy Safety label? — **No** → Congratulations. You are about to risk your life and may be become a pioneer space explorer.

**Yes** → A

---

**A** → Set out to look for food.

Keep walking no matter how tired and hungry you are.

Can you see any form of life? — **No** →

**Yes**

Is it animal? — **No** → Is it vegetable? — **No** → Is it human?

**Yes** → Kill it.   **Yes** → Eat it / Pick it.   **Yes** → Talk to her/him.

Kill it. → Eat it. → Pick it.

Did you check it first in your "Guide to Poisonous Foods in the Galaxy"? — **No** → D

**Yes**

Are you writhing in agony? — **No** → C

**Yes** → Congratulations. You have just discovered the book is inaccurate. → C

Congratulations. You have just discovered the book is inaccurate. → E

Does she/he seem friendly? — **Yes** → B

88

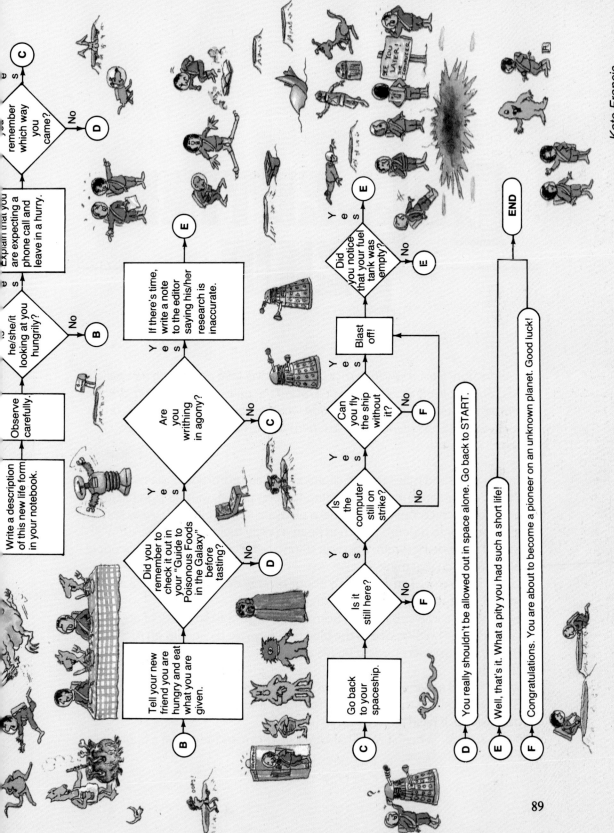

remember which way you came?

C

D — No

...e s

Explain that you are expecting a phone call and leave in a hurry.

...e s — he/she/it looking at you hungrily?

No — B

Observe carefully.

Write a description of this new life form in your notebook.

If there's time, write a note to the editor saying his/her research is inaccurate.

Y e s

E

Are you writhing in agony?

No — C

Y e s

Did you remember to check it out in your "Guide to Poisonous Foods in the Galaxy" before tasting?

No — D

Y e s

Tell your new friend you are hungry and eat what you are given.

B

Did you notice that your fuel tank was empty?

Y e s — E

No — E

Blast off!

Y e s

Can you fly the ship without it?

F — No

Y e s

Is the computer still on strike?

No

Y e s

Is it still here?

No — F

Go back to your spaceship.

C

D → You really shouldn't be allowed out in space alone. Go back to START.

E → Well, that's it. What a pity you had such a short life!

F → Congratulations. You are about to become a pioneer on an unknown planet. Good luck!

END

Kate Francis

89

# COLLECTING TEAM

*This short story lets us see that, most likely, we will take greed with us to alien worlds. The "Collecting Team" hurtles round the galaxies carrying off strange creatures, and seldom stops to question whether they have any right to do so. At least, not until one planet provides them with an unexpected and nasty surprise.*

From fifty thousand miles up, the situation looked promising. It was a middle-sized, brown-and-green, inviting-looking planet, with no sign of cities or any other such complications. Just a pleasant sort of place, the very sort we were looking for to redeem what had been a pretty futile expedition.

I turned to Clyde Holdreth, who was staring reflectively at the thermocouple.

"Well? What do you think?"

"Looks fine to me. Temperature's about seventy down there — nice and warm and plenty of air. I think it's worth a try."

Lee Davison came strolling out from the storage hold smelling of animals, as usual. He was holding one of the blue monkeys we picked up on Alpheraz, and the little beast was crawling up his arm. "Have we found something gentlemen?"

"We've found a planet," I said. "How's the storage space in the hold?"

"Don't worry about that. We've got room for a whole zoo-full more, before we get filled up. It hasn't been a very fruitful trip."

"No," I agreed. "It hasn't. Well? Shall we go down and see what's to be seen?"

"Might as well," Holdreth said. "We can't go back to Earth with just a couple of blue monkeys and some anteaters, you know."

"I'm in favour of a landing too," said Davison. "You?" I nodded. "I'll set up the charts, and you get your animals comfortable for deceleration."

Davison disappeared back into the storage hold, while Holdreth scribbled furiously in the logbook, writing down the co-ordinates of the planet below, its general description, and so forth. Aside from being a collecting team for the zoological department of the Bureau of Interstellar Affairs, we also double as a survey ship, and the planet down below was listed as *unexplored* on our charts.

I glanced out at the mottled brown-and-green ball spinning slowly in the viewport, and felt the warning twinge of gloom that came to me every time we made a landing on a new and strange world. Repressing it, I started to figure out a landing orbit. From behind me came the furious chatter of the blue monkeys as Davison strapped them into their acceleration cradles, and under that the deep, unmusical honking of the Rigelian anteaters, noisily bleating their displeasure.

The planet was inhabited, all right. We hadn't had the ship on the ground more than a minute before the local fauna began to congregate. We stood at the viewport and looked out in wonder.

"This is one of those things you dream about," Davison said, stroking his little beard nervously. "Look at them! There must be a thousand different species out there."

"I've never seen anything like it," said Holdreth.

I computed how much storage space we had left and how many of the thronging creatures outside we would be able to bring back with us. "How are we going to decide what to take and what to leave behind?"

"Does it matter?" Holdreth said gaily. "This is what you call an embarrassment of riches, I guess. We just grab the dozen most bizarre creatures and blast off — and save the rest for another trip. It's too bad we wasted all that time wandering around near Rigel."

"We *did* get the anteaters," Davison pointed out. They were his finds, and he was proud of them.

I smiled sourly. "Yeah. We got the anteaters there." The anteaters honked at that moment, loud and clear. "You know, that's one set of beasts I think I could do without."

"Bad attitude," Holdreth said. "Unprofessional."

"Whoever said I was a zoologist, anyway? I'm just a spaceship pilot, remember. And if I don't like the way those anteaters talk — and — smell — I see no reason why I —"

"Say, look at that one," Davison said suddenly.

I glanced out the viewport and saw a new beast emerging from the thick-packed vegetation in the background. I've seen some fairly strange creatures since I was assigned to the zoological department, but this one took the grand prize.

It was about the size of a giraffe, moving on long, wobbly legs and with a tiny head up at the end of a preposterous neck. Only it had six legs and a bunch of writhing snakelike tentacles as well, and its eyes, great violet globes, stood out nakedly on the ends of two thick stalks. It must have been seven metres high. It moved with exaggerated grace through the swarm of beasts surrounding our ship, pushed its way smoothly towards the vessel, and peered gravely in at the viewport. One purple eye stared directly at me, the other at Davison. Oddly, it seemed to me as if it were trying to tell us something.

"Big one, isn't it?" Davison said finally.

"I'll bet you'd like to bring one back, too."

"Maybe we can fit a young one aboard," Davison said. "If we can find a young one." He turned to Holdreth. "How's that air analysis coming? I'd like to get out there and start collecting. God, that's a crazy-looking beast!"

The animal outside had apparently finished its inspection of us, for it pulled its head away and, gathering its legs under itself, squatted near the ship. A small doglike creature with stiff spines running along its back began to bark at the big creature, which took no notice. The other animals, which came in all shapes and sizes, continued to mill round the ship, evidently very curious about the newcomer to their world. I could see Davison's eyes thirsty with the desire to take the whole kit and caboodle back to Earth with him. I knew what was running through his mind. He was dreaming of the umpteen thousand species of extraterrestrial wildlife roaming around out there, and to each toe he was attaching a neat little tag: *Something-or-other davisoni*.

"The air's fine," Holdreth announced abruptly, looking up from his test-tubes. "Get your butterfly nets and let's see what we can catch."

There was something I didn't like about the place. It was just too good to be true, and I learned long ago that nothing ever is. There's always a catch someplace.

Only this seemed to be on the level. The planet was a bonanza for zoologists, and Davison and Holdreth were having the time of their lives, hipdeep in obliging specimens.

"I've never seen anything like it," Davison said for at least the fiftieth time, as he scooped up a small purplish squirrel-like creature and examined it curiously. The squirrel stared back, examining Davison just as curiously.

"Let's take some of these," Davison said. "I like them."

"Carry 'em on in, then," I said, shrugging. I didn't care which specimens they chose, so long as they filled up the storage hold quickly and let me blast off on schedule. I watched as Davison grabbed a pair of the squirrels and brought them into the ship.

Holdreth came over to me. He was carrying a sort of a dog with insect-faceted eyes and gleaming furless skin. "How's this one, Gus?"

"Fine," I said bleakly. "Wonderful."

He put the animal down — it didn't scamper away, just sat there smiling at us — and looked at me. He ran a hand through his fast-vanishing hair. "Listen, Gus, you've been gloomy all day. What's eating you?"

"I don't like this place," I said.

"Why? Just on general principles?"

"It's too *easy*, Clyde. Much too easy. These animals just flock around here waiting to be picked up."

Holdreth chuckled. "And you're used to a struggle, aren't you? You're just angry at us because we have it so simple here!"

"When I think of the trouble we went through just to get a pair of miserable vile-smelling anteaters, and —"

"Come off it, Gus. We'll load up in a hurry, if you like. But this place is a zoological gold mine!"

I shook my head. "I don't like it, Clyde. Not at all."

Holdreth laughed again and picked up his faceted-eyed dog. "Say, know where I can find another of these, Gus?"

"Right over there," I said, pointing. "By that tree. With its tongue hanging out. It's just waiting to be carried away."

Holdreth looked and smiled. "What do you know about that!" He snared his specimen and carried both of them inside.

I walked away to survey the grounds. The planet was too flatly incredible for me to accept on face value, without at least a look-see, despite the blithe way my two companions were snapping up specimens.

For one thing, animals just don't exist this way — in big miscellaneous quantities, living all together happily. I hadn't noticed more than a few of each kind, and there must have been five hundred different species, each one stranger-looking than the next. Nature doesn't work that way.

For another, they all seemed to be on friendly terms with one another, though they acknowledged the unofficial leadership of the giraffe-like creature. Nature doesn't work that way, either. I hadn't seen one quarrel between the animals yet. That argued that they were all herbivores, which didn't make sense ecologically.

I shrugged my shoulders and walked on.

Half an hour later, I knew a little more about the geography of our bonanza. We were on either an immense island or a peninsula of some sort, because I could see a huge body of water bordering the land some ten miles off. Our vicinity was fairly flat, except for a good-sized hill from which I could see the terrain.

There was a thick, heavily-wooded jungle not too far from the ship. The forest spread out all the way towards the water in one direction, but ended abruptly in the other. We had brought the ship down right at the edge of the clearing. Apparently most of the animals we saw lived in the jungle.

On the other side of our clearing was a low, broad plain that seemed to trail away into a desert in the distance; I could see an uninviting stretch of barren sand that contrasted strangely with the fertile jungle to my left. There was a small lake to the side. It was, I saw, the sort of country likely to attract a varied fauna, since there seemed to be every sort of habitat within a small area.

And the fauna! Although I'm a zoologist only by osmosis, picking up both my interest and my knowledge second-hand from Holdreth and Davison, I couldn't help but be astonished by the wealth of strange animals. They came in all different shapes and sizes, colours and odours, and the only thing they all had in common was their friendliness. During the course of my afternoon's wanderings a hundred animals must have come marching boldly right up to me given me the once-over, and walked away. This included half a dozen kinds that I hadn't seen before, plus one of the eye-stalked, intelligent-looking giraffes and a furless dog. Again, I had the feeling that the giraffe seemed to be trying to communicate.

I didn't like it. I didn't like it at all.

I returned to our clearing, and saw Holdreth and Davison still buzzing madly around, trying to cram as many animals as they could into our hold.

"How's it going?" I asked.

"Hold's all full," Davison said. "We're busy making our alternate selections now." I saw him carrying out Holdreth's two furless dogs and picking up instead a pair of eight-legged penguinish things that uncomplainingly allowed themselves to be carried in. Holdreth was frowning unhappily.

"What do you want *those* for, Lee? Those dog-like ones seem much more interesting, don't you think?"

"No," Davison said. "I'd rather bring along these two. They're curious beasts, aren't they? Look at the muscular network that connects the —"

"Hold it, fellows," I said. I peered at the animal in Davison's hands and glanced up. "This is a curious beast," I said. "It's got eight legs."

"You becoming a zoologist?" Holdreth asked, amused.

"No — but I am getting puzzled. Why should this one have eight legs, some of the others here six, and some of the others only four?"

They looked at me blankly, with the scorn of professionals.

"I mean, there ought to be some sort of logic to evolution here, shouldn't there? On Earth we've developed a four-legged pattern of animal life; on Venus, they usually run to six legs. But have you ever seen an evolutionary hodgepodge like this place before?"

"There are stranger setups," Holdreth said. "The symbiotes on Sirius Three, the burrowers of Mizar — but you're right, Gus. This is a peculiar evolutionary dispersal. I think we ought to stay and investigate it fully."

Instantly I knew from the bright expression on Davison's face that I had blundered, had made things worse than ever. I decided to take a new tack.

"I don't agree," I said. "I think we ought to leave with what we've got, and come back with a larger expedition later."

Davison chuckled. "Come on, Gus, don't be silly! This is a chance of a lifetime for us — why should we call in the whole zoological department on it?"

I didn't want to tell them I was afraid of staying longer. I crossed my arms. "Lee, I'm the pilot of this ship, and you'll have to listen to me. The schedule calls for a brief stopover here, and we have to leave. Don't tell me I'm being silly."

"But you are, man! You're standing blindly in the path of scientific investigation, of —"

"Listen to me, Lee. Our food is calculated on a pretty narrow margin, to allow you fellows more room for storage. And this is strictly a collecting team.

There's no provision for extended stays on any one planet. Unless you want to wind up eating your own specimens, I suggest you allow me to get out of here."

They were silent for a moment. Then Holdreth said, "I guess we can't argue with that, Lee. Let's listen to Gus and go back now. There's plenty of time to investigate this place later when we can take longer."

"But — oh, all right," Davison said reluctantly. He picked up the eight-legged penguins. "Let me stash these things in the hold, and we can leave." He looked strangely at me, as if I had done something criminal.

As he started into the ship, I called to him.

"What is it, Gus?"

"Look here, Lee. I don't *want* to pull you away from here. It's simply a matter of food," I lied, masking my nebulous suspicions.

"I know how it is, Gus." He turned and entered the ship.

I stood there thinking about nothing at all for a moment, then went inside myself to begin setting up the blastoff orbit.

I got as far as calculating the fuel expenditure when I noticed something. Feedwires were dangling crazily down from the control cabinet. Somebody had wrecked our drive mechanism, but thoroughly.

For a long moment, I stared stiffly at the sabotaged drive. Then I turned and headed into the storage hold.

"Davison?"

"What is it, Gus?"

"Come out here a second, will you?"

I waited, and a few minutes later he appeared, frowning impatiently. "What do you want, Gus? I'm busy and I —" His mouth dropped open. "*Look at the drive!*"

"You look at it," I snapped. "I'm sick. Go get Holdreth, on the double."

While he was gone I tinkered with the shattered mechanism. Once I had the cabinet panel off and could see the inside, I felt a little better; the drive wasn't damaged beyond repair, though it had been pretty well scrambled. Three or four days of hard work with a screwdriver and solderbeam might get the ship back into functioning order.

But that didn't make me any less angry. I heard Holdreth and Davison entering behind me, and I whirled to face them.

"All right, you idiots. Which one of you did this?"

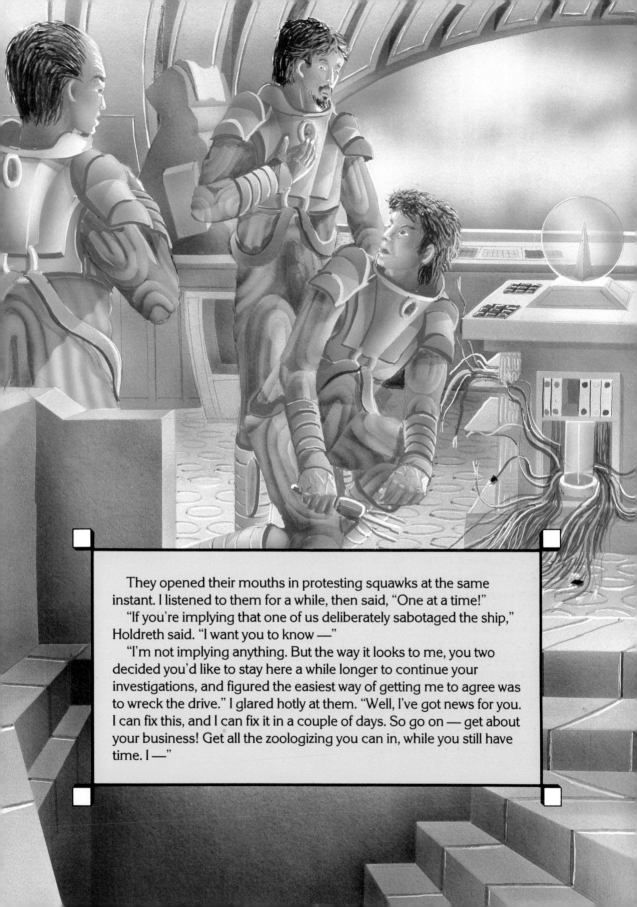

They opened their mouths in protesting squawks at the same instant. I listened to them for a while, then said, "One at a time!"

"If you're implying that one of us deliberately sabotaged the ship," Holdreth said. "I want you to know —"

"I'm not implying anything. But the way it looks to me, you two decided you'd like to stay here a while longer to continue your investigations, and figured the easiest way of getting me to agree was to wreck the drive." I glared hotly at them. "Well, I've got news for you. I can fix this, and I can fix it in a couple of days. So go on — get about your business! Get all the zoologizing you can in, while you still have time. I —"

Davison laid a hand gently on my arm. "Gus," he said quietly, "*We didn't do it.* Neither of us."

Suddenly all the anger drained out of me and was replaced by raw fear. I could see that Davison meant it.

"If you didn't do it, and Holdreth didn't do it, and I didn't do it — then who did?"

Davison shrugged.

"Maybe it's one of us who doesn't know he's doing it," I suggested. "Maybe —" I stopped. "Oh, that's nonsense. Hand me that tool-kit, will you, Lee?"

They left to tend to the animals, and I set to work on the repair job, dismissing all further speculations and suspicions from my mind, concentrating solely on joining, Lead A to Input A and Transistor F to Potentiometer K, as indicated. It was slow, nerve-harrowing work, and by mealtime I had accomplished only the barest preliminaries. My fingers were starting to quiver from the strain of small-scale work, and I decided to give up the job for the day and get back to it tomorrow.

I slept uneasily, my nightmares punctuated by the moaning of the accursed anteaters and the occasional squeals, chuckles, bleats, and hisses of the various other creatures in the hold. It must have been four in the morning before I dropped off into a really sound sleep, and what was left of the night passed swiftly. The next thing I knew, hands were shaking me and I was looking up into the pale, tense faces of Holdreth and Davison.

I pushed my sleep-stuck eyes open and blinked. "Huh? What's going on?"

Holdreth leaned down and shook me savagely. "Get up, Gus!"

I struggled to my feet slowly. "Hell of a thing to do, wake a fellow up in the middle of the —"

I found myself being propelled from my cabin and led down the corridor to the control room. Blearily, I followed where Holdreth pointed, and then I woke up in a hurry.

The drive was battered again. Someone — or *something* — had completely undone my repair job of the night before.

If there had been bickering among us, it stopped. This was past the category of a joke now; it couldn't be laughed off, and we found ourselves working together as a tight unit again, trying desperately to solve the puzzle before it was too late.

"Let's review the situation," Holdreth said, pacing nervously up and down the control cabin. "The drive has been sabotaged twice. None of us knows who did it, and on a conscious level each of us is convinced *he* didn't do it."

He paused. "That leaves us with two possibilities. Either, as Gus suggested, one of us is doing it unaware of it even himself, or someone else is doing it while we're not looking. Neither possibility is a very cheerful one."

"We can stay on guard, though," I said. "Here's what I propose; first, have one of us awake at all times — sleep in shifts, that is, with somebody guarding the drive until I get it fixed. Two — jettison all the animals aboard ship."

"*What?*"

"He's right," Davison said. "We don't know what we may have brought aboard. They don't seem to be intelligent, but we can't be sure. That purple-eyed baby giraffe, for instance — suppose he's been hypnotizing us into damaging the drive ourselves? How can we tell?"

"Oh, but —" Holdreth started to protest, then stopped and frowned soberly. "I suppose we'll have to admit the possibility," he said, obviously unhappy about the prospect of freeing our captives. "We'll empty out the hold, and you see if you can get the drive fixed. Maybe later we'll recapture them all, if nothing further develops."

We agreed to that, and Holdreth and Davison cleared the ship of its animal cargo while I set to work determinedly at the drive mechanism. By nightfall, I had managed to accomplish as much as I had the day before.

I sat up as watch the first shift, aboard the strangely quiet ship. I paced around the drive cabin, fighting the great temptation to doze off, and managed to last through until the time Holdreth arrived to relieve me.

Only — when he showed up, he gasped and pointed at the drive. It had been ripped apart a third time.

Now we had no excuse, no explanation. The expedition had turned into a nightmare.

I could only protest that I had remained awake my entire spell on duty, and that I had seen no one and nothing approach the drive panel. But that was hardly a satisfactory explanation, since it either cast guilt on me as the saboteur or implied that some unseen external power was repeatedly wrecking the drive. Neither hypothesis made sense, at least to me.

By now we had spent four days on the planet, and food was getting to be a major problem. My carefully budgeted flight schedule called for us to be two days out on our return journey to Earth by now. But we still were no closer to departure than we had been four days ago.

The animals continued to wander around outside, nosing up against the ship, examining it, almost fondling it, with those damned pseudo-giraffes staring soulfully at us always. The beasts were as friendly as ever, little knowing how the tension was growing within the hull. The three of us walked around like zombies, eyes bright and lips clamped. We were scared — all of us.

Something was keeping us from fixing the drive.

Something didn't want us to leave this planet.

I looked at the bland face of the purple-eyed giraffe staring through the viewport, and it stared mildly back at me. Around it was grouped the rest of the local fauna, the same incredible hodgepodge of improbable genera and species.

That night, the three of us stood guard in the control-room together. The drive was smashed anyway. The wires were soldered in so many places by now that the control panel was a mass of shining alloy, and I knew that a few more such sabotagings and it would be impossible to patch it together any more — if it wasn't so already.

The next night, I just didn't knock off. I continued soldering right on after dinner (and a pretty skimpy dinner it was, now that we were on close rations) and far on into the night.

By morning, it was as if I hadn't done a thing.

"I give up," I announced, surveying the damage. "I don't see any sense in ruining my nerves trying to fix a thing that won't stay fixed."

Holdreth nodded. He looked terribly pale. "We'll have to find some new approach."

"Yeah. Some new approach."

I yanked open the food closet and examined our stock. Even figuring in the synthetics we would have fed to the animals if we hadn't released them, we were low on food. We had overstayed even the safety margin. It would be a hungry trip back — if we ever did get back.

I clambered through the hatch and sprawled down on a big rock near the ship. One of the furless dogs came over and nuzzled in my shirt. Davison stepped to the hatch and called down to me.

"What are you doing out there, Gus?"

"Just getting a little fresh air. I'm sick of living aboard that ship." I scratched the dog behind his pointed ears, and looked around.

The animals had lost most of their curiosity about us, and didn't congregate the way they used to. They were meandering all over the plain, nibbling at little deposits of a white doughy substance. It precipitated every night. "Manna", we called it. All the animals seemed to live on it.

I folded my arms and leaned back.

We were getting to look awfully lean by the eighth day. I wasn't even trying to fix the ship any more; the hunger was starting to get me. But I saw Davison puttering around with my solderbeam.

"What are you doing?"

"I'm going to repair the drive," he said. "You don't want to, but we can't just sit around, you know." His nose was deep in my repair guide, and he was fumbling with the release on the solderbeam.

I shrugged. "Go ahead, if you want to." I didn't care what he did. All I cared about was the gaping emptiness in my stomach, and about the dimly grasped fact that somehow we were stuck here for good.

"Gus?"

"Yeah?"

"I think it's time I told you something. I've been eating the manna for four days. It's good. It's nourishing stuff."

"You've been eating — the manna? Something that grows on an alien world? You crazy?"

"What else can we do? Starve?"

I smiled feebly, admitting that he was right. From somewhere in the back of the ship came the sounds of Holdreth moving around. Holdreth had taken this thing worse than any of us. He had a family back on Earth, and he was beginning to realize that he wasn't ever going to see them again.

"Why don't you get Holdreth?" Davison suggested. "Go out there and stuff yourselves with the manna. You've got to eat something."

"Yeah. What can I lose?" Moving like a mechanical man, I headed towards Holdreth's cabin. We would go out and eat the manna and cease being hungry, one way or another.

"Clyde?" I called. "Clyde?"

I entered his cabin. He was sitting at his desk, shaking convulsively, staring at the two streams of blood that trickled in red spurts from his slashed wrists.

"*Clyde!*"

He made no protest as I dragged him towards the infirmary cabin and got tourniquets around his arms, cutting off the bleeding. He just stared dully ahead, sobbing.

I slapped him and he came around. He shook his head dizzily, as if he didn't know where he was.

"I — I —"

"Easy, Clyde. Everything's all right."

"It's *not* all right," he said hollowly. "I'm still alive. Why didn't you let me die? Why didn't you —"

Davison entered the cabin. "What's been happening, Gus?"

"It's Clyde. The pressure's getting him. He tried to kill himself, but I think he's all right now. Get him something to eat, will you?"

We had Holdreth straightened around by evening. Davison gathered as much of the manna as he could find, and we held a feast.

"I wish we had nerve enough to kill some of the local fauna," Davison said. "Then we'd have a feast — steaks and everything!"

"The bacteria," Holdreth pointed out quietly. "We don't dare."

"I know. But it's a thought."

"No more thoughts," I said sharply. "Tomorrow morning we start work on the drive panel again. Maybe with some food in our bellies we'll be able to keep awake and see what's happening here."

Holdreth smiled. "Good. I can't wait to get out of this ship and back to a normal existence. God, I just can't wait!"

"Let's get some sleep," I said. "Tomorrow we'll give it another try. We'll get back," I said with a confidence I didn't feel.

The following morning I rose early and got my tool-kit. My head was clear, and I was trying to put the pieces together without much luck. I started towards the control cabin.

And stopped.

And looked out the viewport.

I went back and awoke Holdreth and Davison. "Take a look out the port," I said hoarsely.

They looked. They gaped.

"It looks just like my house," Holdreth said. "My house on Earth."

"With all the comforts of home inside, I'll bet." I walked forward uneasily and lowered myself through the hatch. "Let's go look at it."

We approached it, while the animals frolicked around us. The big giraffe came near and shook its head gravely. The house stood in the middle of the clearing, small and neat and freshly-painted.

I saw it now. During the night, invisible hands had put it there. Had assembled and built a cosy little Earth-type house and dropped it next to our ship for us to live in.

"Just like my house," Holdreth repeated in wonderment.

"It should be," I said. "They grabbed the model from your mind, as soon as they found out we couldn't live on the ship indefinitely."

Holdreth and Davison asked as one, "What do you mean?"

"You mean you haven't figured this place out yet?" I licked my lips, getting myself used to the fact that I was going to spend the rest of my life here. "You mean you don't realize what this house is intended to be?"

They shook their heads, baffled. I glanced around, from the house to the useless ship to the jungle to the plain to the little pond. It all made sense now.

"They want to keep us happy," I said. "They knew we weren't thriving aboard the ship, so they — they built us something a little more like home."

"They? The giraffes?"

"Forget the giraffes. They tried to warn us, but it's too late. They're intelligent beings, but they're prisoners just like us. I'm talking about the ones who run this place. The super-aliens who make us sabotage our own ship and not even know we're doing it, who stand someplace up there and gape at us. The ones who dredged together this motley assortment of beasts from all over the galaxy. Now we've been collected too. This whole damned place is just a zoo — a zoo for aliens so far ahead of us we don't dare dream what they're like."

I looked up at the shimmering blue-green sky, where invisible bars seemed to restrain us, and sank down dismally on the porch of our new home. I was resigned. There wasn't any sense in struggling against them.

I could see the neat little placard now:

EARTHMEN. Native Habitat, Sol III.

*Written by Robert Silverberg*
*Illustrated by Peter Schmidli*

# HERE IS THE NEWS FROM SPACE

The Space News Agency Atmos report
that the sun can be seen quite a lot
these days,
but not very much
at night.

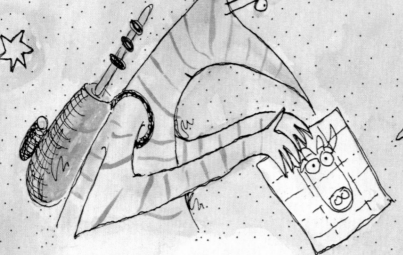

The spokesman in the moon said:
"Hey diddle diddle
the cat and the fiddle
the cow jumped over the moon.
The little dog laughed
to see such fun
and the dish ran away with the spoon."

Venus police have issued identikit pictures
of the cat and the cow, and
a dish is being held for questioning.
Police have put out a special appeal
for any little dog at or near the moon
at the time
to come forward and help with further investigation
of the affair.

*Michael Rosen*

# S-P-A-C-E-D

## words Glossary

**agitated** (*p.62*)
disturbed, troubled

**anguish** (*p.16*)
distress, worry, misery

**asymmetrically** (*p.54*)
not symmetrically

**atrium** (*p.48*)
the courtyard of a
Roman house

**carbide** (*p.10*)
the strong smell of
carbon gas

**cleft** (*p.13*)
split or crack between
large areas of rock

**convulsively** (*p.107*)
jerkily, violently

**cumbersome** (*p.84*)
bulky and heavy

**defiantly** (*p.38*)
boldly without fear

**detonation** (*p.19*)
explosion

**distraught** (*p.66*)
agitated, very upset

**ecologically** (*p.98*)
according to the
pattern of living things
connected to their
surroundings

**elated** (*p.13*)
in high spirits

**endeavour** (*p.64*)
attempt, try

**fauna** (*p.98*)
animal life

**futile** (*p.90*)
useless

**gorges** (*p.13*)
narrow valleys through
the land

**grotesque** (*p.38*)
deformed, ugly or
twisted in a strange
shape

**herbivores** (*p.98*)
plant-eating animals

**hypothesis** (*p.103*)
explanation

**immune** (*p.19*)
protected against

**Inquisition monks** (*p.6*)
monks belonging to
the Roman Catholic
Church (1232–1830)
who questioned and
often tortured people
who did not believe in
God

**insect faceted** (*p.95*)
like the eye of an
insect, made up of
many separate units

**instantaneously** (*p.51*)
at almost the same time

**interminable** (*p.49*)
endless

**meandering** (*p.106*)
wandering

**miscellaneous** (*p.95*)
various

Glossary continues on page 112

**monotony** *(p.54)*
boring repetition

**morepork** *(p.16)*
a nocturnal Australian
bird

**nebulous** *(p.100)*
vague

**osmosis** *(p.98)*
passing of one thing to
another

**perimeter** *(p.46)*
outer edge or limits of
something

**pewter** *(p.10)*
a dull bluish-grey
colour

**ponderously** *(p.17)*
slowly, heavily

**posture** *(p.54)*
the way of holding the
body

**purify** *(p.22)*
make clean

**ravines** *(p.13)*
narrow steep-sided
valleys

**recruited** *(p.50)*
enrolled, taken on as
members of a group

**redeem** *(p.90)*
save

**rehabilitation** *(p.54)*
adapting or getting
used to a new situation
or way of life

**rheostat** *(p.54)*
instrument used to
control electrical
currents

**sabotaged** *(p.100)*
deliberately destroyed
or damaged property
(usually done secretly)

**satyr** *(p.49)*
mythical Roman
creature — goat-like
man

**telepathic** *(p.65)*
able to communicate
thoughts or feelings
without speaking

**triclinium** *(p.48)*
three couches grouped
around a dining table
(the Romans usually
lay down when eating)

**vicinity** *(p.98)*
surrounding area